CHRISTMAS IN NEW YORK

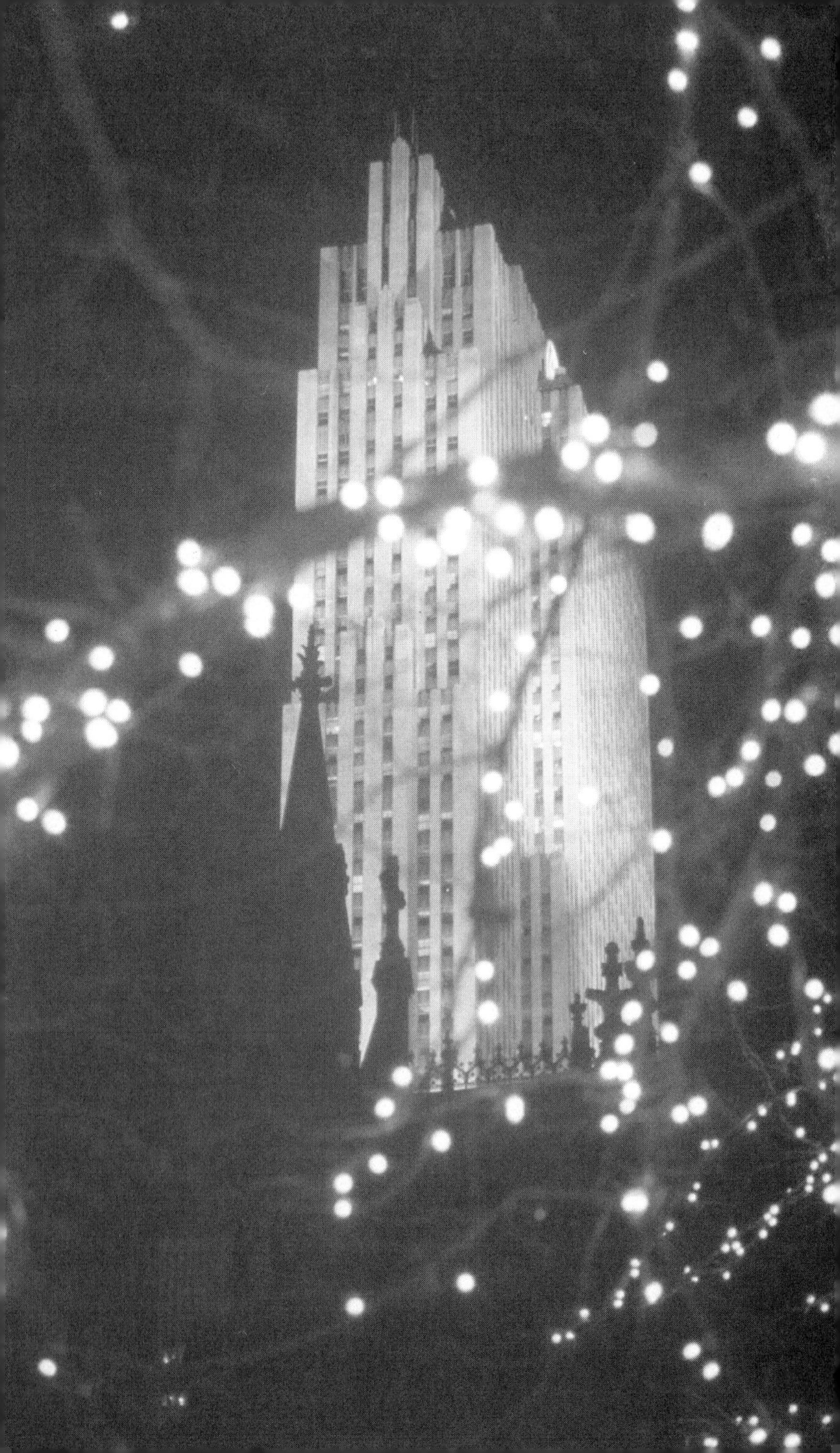

CHRISTMAS IN
NEW YORK

DANIEL POOL

Seven Stories Press / New York

In the U.K.: Turnaround Publisher Services Ltd., Unit 3, Olympia Trading
Estate, Coburg Road, Wood Green, London N22 6TZ U.K.

In Canada: Hushion House, 36 Northline Road, Toronto, Ontario M4B
3E2, Canada

Library of Congress Cataloging-in-Publication Data
Pool, Daniel.
    Christmas in New York / Daniel Pool. — 1st ed.
    p. cm.
    ISBN 1-888363-55-X
    1. Christmas—New York (State)—New York. 2. New York (N.Y.)—
Social life and customs. I. Title.
GT4986.N7P66 1997
394.2663'09747—dc21   97-24779
                                          CIP

Book design by Cindy LaBreacht

Frontispiece: Rockefeller Center's GE Building seen from
St. Patrick's Cathedral. Title page: Thomas Nast's Santa Claus.
Page 6: Manhattan's Municipal Building.
Page 8: The Rockefeller Center Christmas Tree.

Seven Stories Press
632 Broadway, 7th Floor
New York, NY 10012

Printed in the U.S.A.
9 8 7 6 5 4 3 2 1

For Eileen

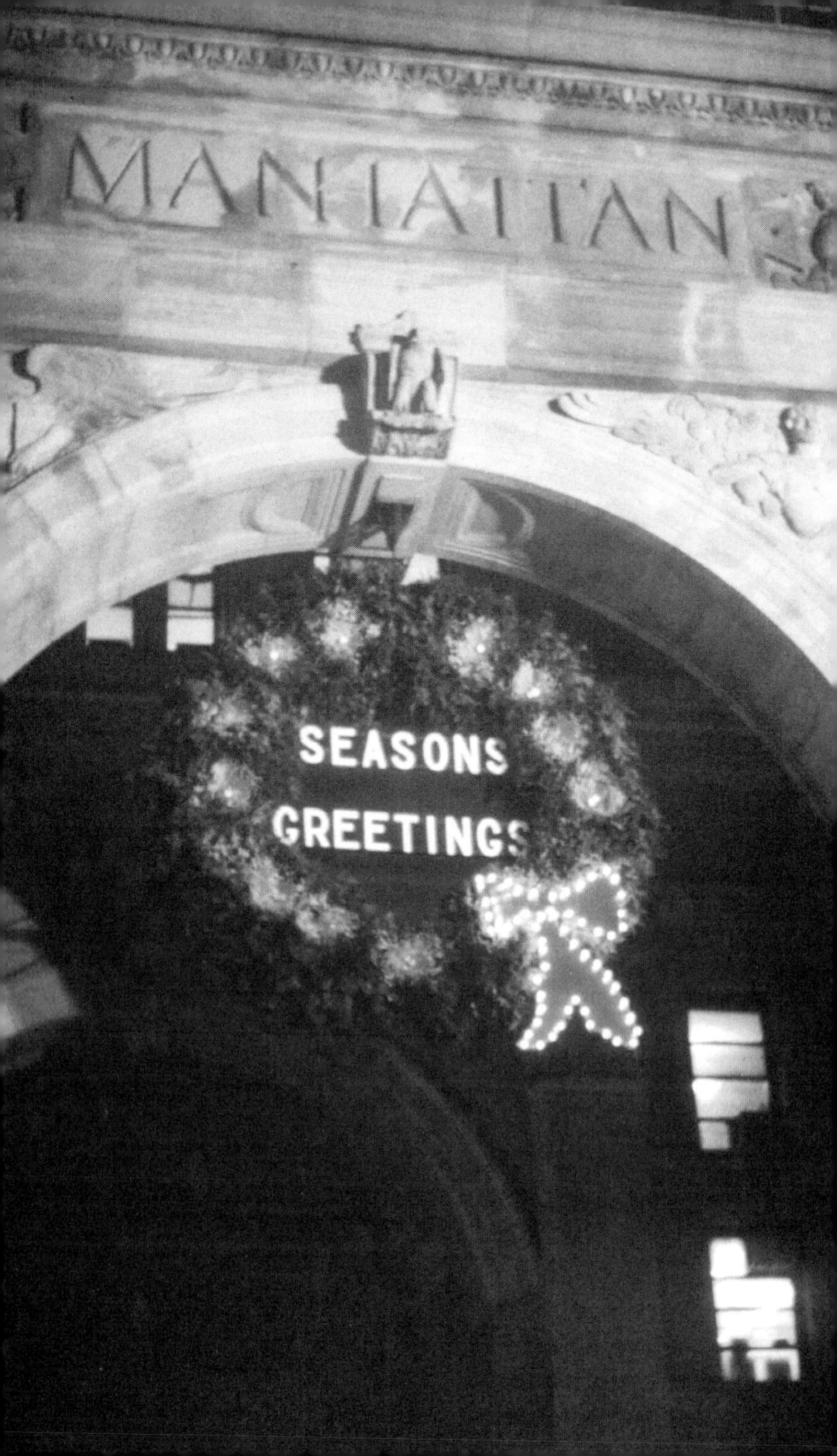
MANHATTAN
SEASONS
GREETINGS

CONTENTS

It is Christmas in New York.

During the day, stores are crowded, traffic is snarled, hordes of people surge down Fifth Avenue to view the Rockefeller Center tree, the theaters are jammed, and festive mega-budget films of eye-gouging and dismemberment announce the arrival of the holiday film season. When New York decides to put on the dog, dress up and do the holiday version of its bright-lights, big-city number, it can dazzle mightily. But, then after all, New York invented electric Christmas tree lights, Lionel trains, F.A.O. Schwarz, "White Christmas," and—oh, yes—Santa Claus...

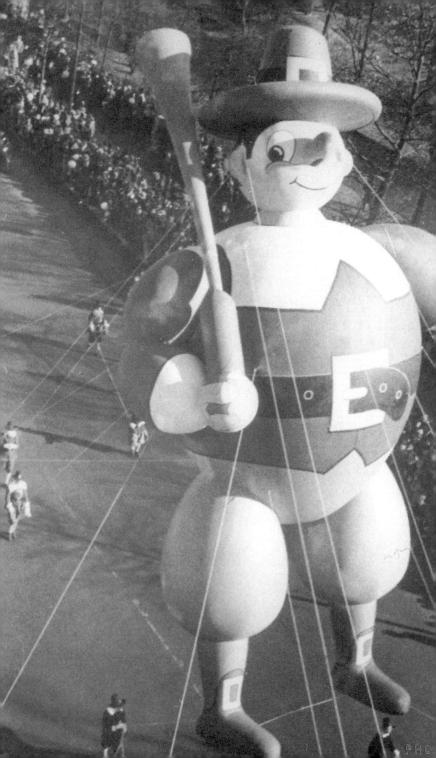

Macy's Thanksgiving Day Parade

I n New York nowadays the Christmas season begins with the Macy's Thanksgiving Day parade, which in 1996 consisted of thirty-one floats, forty-one giant balloons, and thirteen marching bands (all chaperoned by over four thousand Macy's employees, plus twelve hundred balloon wranglers) and which is, let's face it, an effort by Macy's to pre-empt customers for itself in the Christmas rush, a crucial period of a few weeks during which a big store often does thirty percent of its entire annual business.

Macy's Thanksgiving Day Balloon, 1946.

Macy's store was started at 204 Sixth Avenue in 1858 by bearded, tattooed (on the back of his hands) former whaling man and smoker of black cigars Rowland Macy, "dealer in Dry Goods, Carpets, Oil Clothes, Matting, &c," as the sign said. Macy's has been a Christmas stalwart for years. It was open Christmas Eve till midnight back in *1867*; began selling toys in 1869; provided same-day delivery on Christmas Eve beginning in the 1880s with its fleet of horses and wagons; and introduced Christmas gift certificates in 1906. When the store was still located at 14th Street and Sixth Avenue, the ground floor of Macy's would be cleared out around December 15 and devoted entirely to toys, one year including a mechanical singing bird from

*M*ACY'S EMPLOYEES ESCORTING THANKSGIVING DAY
PARADE FLOAT, CIRCA 1924.

HOLIDAY PASSERSBY ADMIRING MACY'S
DISPLAY WINDOWS IN THE 1880s.

Europe that drew repeated visits from Mr. Macy's pal P.T. Barnum. (Store mannequins then were lifelike wax figures, and some of the early Macy's Christmas window displays in the late 1800s were built by the Eden Musée, a wax museum at 23rd Street and Sixth Avenue that featured a chess-playing automaton and a Chamber of Horrors.)

In 1902, Macy's moved uptown to a vast new store at 34th Street and Herald Square. Macy's continued to grow. In the early 1920s, Macy's doubled its already large floor space to 1.5 million square feet. It put up an electric sign with the city's biggest letters and inaugurated a gigantic new display window, sixty feet long and nine feet deep, with a special preview, as if it were a theater opening. But if you built it, would they come? Could the store draw enough additional shoppers for the crucial Christmas season to justify this massive expansion?

There was already a tradition of Thanksgiving pageantry and revelry in New York City. "Thanksgiving Day in the Lower East Side," former governor Al Smith recalled in 1929 of the old days, "provided amusement for the people by a parade of what are still called ragamuffins." On Thanksgiving Day before that, there had been parades of "fantasticals," neighborhood groups of working class men who dressed up in costume, giving themselves bizarre names like the Gilhooley Musketeers, the Original Hounds Guard, or the Secondhand Lumberdealers Association. True "fantasticals" began Thanksgiving with blasts on a fish horn to wake all New York. "Captain Kyd sat in a coach with Bismarck, Wah Kee, and the Duke of Cherry Hill," noted the *New York Times* in 1881 of a group of some 150 costumed revellers gathered under the aegis of the Squareback Rangers outside a Lower East Side saloon preparatory to a day of carousing, and "behind them was a man wearing a woman's riding habit" going by the name of "Mrs. Vanderbilt." The Squarebacks paraded uptown, picnicking in the afternoon and closing the day with a spectacular ball in a celebration whose collateral descendants survive to this day in the carryings on of the Philadelphia Mummers or the Mardi Gras. But Thanksgiving was not just for adults. It was also known as

"Ragamuffin Day," because children all around the city dressed up, Halloween-style, in rags and went begging, the girls very often costumed as boys and vice versa, a custom that may go back to when the city was a Dutch settlement.

Parades? Costumes? In devising a holiday attention-getter, Macy's could also draw on a specifically commercial variety of parade that was then a common feature of American life. Traditionally when the circus came into town, a parade of animals and colorfully costumed performers served as a means to advertise the show's wonders. The parade pulled the crowd along after the procession to the place where the tents were finally pitched—and where tickets were sold to the show. In the Twenties, the big department stores instituted circus-like parades for which they simply substituted the store for the circus tent as a destination.

Gimbel's of Philadelphia pioneered this kind of parade in the early 1920s with fifteen cars and a fireman who agreed to dress as Santa, and Macy's followed suit with its first Thanksgiving parade on November 27, 1924. Accompanied by Macy's employees dressed—like the "fantasticals"—as knights, clowns and such, the parade began at 145th Street and Convent Avenue in northern Manhattan, wound its way down Morningside and Manhattan Avenues, turned west onto Broadway at 110th Street, went down

Broadway to Columbus Circle, then down Eighth Avenue to 40th Street, then east to Broadway again. Hours later it finally staggered into Herald Square, where Santa was crowned "King of the Kiddies" in front of the store. He then pulled a string to unveil the store's Christmas display win-

NEW YORK CHILDREN DRESSED UP TO BEG ON "RAGAMUFFIN DAY," I.E. THANKSGIVING.

dows as shoppers rushed the store. "There also were bears, elephants, donkeys, and bands," said the *Times*, "making the procession resemble a circus parade," which was the whole point, of course. (The animals were borrowed from the Central Park Zoo.)

Lions and tigers were added the next year, and there was a massive 100-foot-long caterpillar float that bobbed and stumbled and weaved down Broadway. In 1926, Macy's shortened the parade so that it started at Broadway and 110th Street. The parade was already so popular that Macy's Santa was drawing 5,000 children a day to 34th Street and had to be moved to a new location in the store. In fact, patriotic groups protested that the parade kept people from the then customary morning church services, so the store for a time moved it to the afternoon.

But there was a more serious problem. The living, breathing wild animals were simply too scary for many little children, and steers featured in the parade panicked and stampeded through the city. What to do? To the rescue came a stocky puppeteer named Tony Sarg, who had created Macy's Christmas window displays and had designed the floats for the first Macy's parade. The son of a German sugar and coffee planter in Guatemala who tried to force him into a career in the German military, Sarg fled to England. There he taught himself puppetry and put on shows that drew applause from no less a personage than George Bernard Shaw. Sarg came to the United States in 1915 and set up a studio on the top floor of the Flatiron building. He did much to single-handedly revive the dying art of puppetry in the United States, training, among others, Bil Baird, who devised the puppets that accompany the song "The Lonely Goatherd" in the film *The Sound of Music*.

In 1927, Sarg replaced the parade's wild animals with artificial beasts—giant papier-mâché figures—including a sixty-foot dinosaur and a twenty-five foot long dachshund. The next year inspiration turned to genius. Sarg replaced the giant papier-mâché animals in turn with creatures made of helium-filled balloons. They were a natural invention for a puppeteer since, as Bil Baird said, they were "simply upside-down marionettes manipulated from strings underneath rather than above." Moreover, in an age when the dirigible and zeppelin were popular, making use of large blimp-like inflatables was a rather trendy idea. So there were quickly stitched together for the parade with the help of the Goodyear tire company, which had acquired a zeppelin division in 1924, a dragon, Felix the Cat, a toy soldier, and an elephant.

In a dramatic gesture at the parade's end, the huge balloons were *released* into the sky, with the promise of a $15 reward to each finder. (The helium expanded and the bal-

TONY SARG, INVENTOR OF THE MACY'S THANKSGIVING
DAY PARADE BALLOONS.

loons burst as they rose, so in 1929 safety valves were installed on them.) In 1930, there were fifteen giant figures, including a Katzenjammer Kid that was whisked by the wind up to the 70th story of the Empire State Building, where the Kid leered out at the crowd for a moment, then "moved to the corner," a *Times* reporter noted, and "slowly seemed to peer round it," after which the wind snatched it off and away.

The giant balloons continued to be released at the parade's end each year until 1932. That year a giant cat that had been freed soared up 5,000 feet into a biplane being piloted over Jamaica Bay by student pilot Annette Gibson of Brooklyn, almost killing her and her instructor. Another giant balloon drifted out to sea, and the Coast Guard reported anxious queries from ships in the mid-Atlantic about strange sea creatures that had been sighted. Moreover, two tugs fighting to recover a dachshund balloon from the East River tore the dog apart. So, starting in 1934, the giant balloons were quietly deflated after each parade. The store released thousands of small balloons instead, 200 of them with special tags that entitled the finder to $1 worth of free merchandise at Macy's. Over the years the store's balloons floated as far away as Pittsburgh, Baltimore, and Nova Scotia.

The star of the 1934 parade was the vastly popular singer and radio personality Eddie Cantor, in whose likeness a balloon was created that year, the only time a real human being has been so honored. When Santa and the parade reached Macy's, Cantor warbled a curious song which he was currently introducing to the nation on his radio show. "You better watch out, You better not cry…," he sang, from—yes—"Santa Claus Is Comin' To Town," a song written that very year by Tin Pan Alley writers *par excellence* J. Fred Coots (music) and Haven Gillespie (words).

"I wrote the lyrics at the end of a bar in fifteen minutes on the back of an envelope," cheerfully recalled Gillespie. He was a Kentucky boy who had left high school to become a printer and journeyman (for a while he worked for the *New York Times*) and then quit to write songs. Coots, a song plugger, was a vaudeville writer and performer from Brooklyn who wrote for Sophie Tucker and also turned out material for musicals under contract to the Shubert brothers (as in the Shubert organization). More important, he was writing songs for Cantor's weekly radio show in 1934, and he prevailed on the singer's wife, Ida, to have Eddie perform "Santa Claus Is Comin' To Town" on the air after Cantor originally turned it down as a "kiddie song." It was an immediate hit. By 1964, when *Newsweek* did a "Where Are They Now?" about the two songwriters, "Santa" had sold over 70 million records.

For some years the traditional aspects of Thanksgiving peculiar to New York, notably "Ragamuffin Day's" costumed begging, lingered figuratively and literally alongside the new parade. "A boy in a jacket of mink, rouged lips, and high heels, approached one of the patrolmen directing the start of the Macy parade near the Cathedral of St. John the Divine," recorded the *Herald Tribune* in 1934. "With a Mae West shimmy and an inviting smile he said: 'Come up and see me some time.' The policeman looked astonished, stared closely, then switched the cord of his night-stick sharply against the youngster's legs and growled: 'Get out of here. Come on, beat it.' In front of the Paramount Building in Times Square several score persons crowded around three little hoydens in boys' clothes who were singing and dancing for pennies." By the end of World War II, however, "Ragamuffin Day" had virtually disappeared from the city.

The war brought other changes, including a rubber shortage. In 1942 on the steps of City Hall Macy's president ceremonially presented Mayor LaGuardia with a dragon balloon—and a dagger—with which LaGuardia slew the inflated beast, and the store then donated 650 pounds of rubber to the war effort. There was no parade that year, the following year, or in 1944. After the war, the start of the parade was moved down to its present point of origin at 77th Street. It is there, behind the Museum of

Natural History the night before each parade, that the five-
to six-story-high balloons are now "inflated." (This has been
the preferred term ever since a Goodyear executive panicked years ago when he tuned in the parade on his radio
only to hear the announcer say excitedly, "And now the balloons are all blown up!") The parade was nationally televised for the first time in 1948 (the last year, incidentally,
that the store gave a free Thanksgiving turkey to each of
its employees), and in 1995 it drew an estimated 60 million viewers.

The commercialism of today's parade is nothing new.
At the turn of the century the *New York Tribune* noted darkly
that "as soon as the Thanksgiving turkey is eaten, the great
question of buying Christmas presents begins to take the
terrifying shape it has come to assume in recent years." "40-
Ft. Rodent, Followed By 50-Ft. Eddie Cantor Too Much
for Police Horses" said the *Herald Tribune* sardonically of the
1934 parade, alluding to the fact that what rescued many
toymakers and movie theaters from oblivion in the Thirties was the immense popularity of the then brand-new
Mickey Mouse. Seventeen out of the 25 parade balloons
in 1995 were licensed figures whom sponsors paid Macy's
to put in the parade. In recent years, toymakers have paid
Macy's up to $350,000 a balloon to advertise their lead-
ing characters and toys—which is perhaps one reason why,

when one of the sponsored balloons got punctured and deflated during the 1995 parade, television cameras unobtrusively (and silently) cut to footage of the same balloon that had been filmed the day before.

The parade has grappled with adversity before, of course. In 1941, a Santa balloon burst as it was being inflated; in 1956, 45 mile per hour winds knocked all but one balloon out of commission by the end of the parade; in 1958 air-filled balloons had to be carried along the parade route suspended from cranes because of a national helium shortage; and because of high winds in 1971 there were no balloons at all in the parade. Winds have not yet carried off any balloon wranglers, although the balloons can exert up to 600 pounds of vertical lift. The wranglers must each weigh at least 125 pounds, and they work the balloons in groups.

Tiny models of the parade's balloons are built across the river in Hoboken, New Jersey. From the miniatures full size balloons are then constructed of extra-tough urethane-coated nylon. They are divided internally into separate air-tight compartments so that if one compartment deflates the whole balloon doesn't die. And the figures will stay upright as they are pulled along during the parade because while helium is pumped into the top compartments, the compartments in the bottom of each figure contain mostly air, which is heavier than helium. At midnight on Thanksgiving Eve a police escort shepherds the floats for the parade through a tube of the Lincoln Tunnel closed especially for the occasion and at 3 a.m.——yes, *3 a.m.*——the bands that will march later that morning practice down at 34th Street. Streets along the parade route are cleared of broken glass, lamp posts are bent back out of the way, and trees, if necessary, are pruned so broken branches cannot puncture any balloons. And then, come Thanksgiving morning at 9 a.m., the signal is given, the costumed and uniformed marchers step out——and once again the valiant employees start down Central Park West along the two-and-a-half mile parade route with their giant charges, struggling to control the balloons that, like everything else in Manhattan, have a mind of their own.

A Holiday Walk Along Fifth Avenue

The Macy's parade is, in one sense, a fitting start to Christmas in New York, because Christmas in the Big Apple is really all about spectacle. Spectacle in the sense of colorfully dressed, bustling crowds of sight-seers and shoppers, holiday films and theater, decorated buildings and special holiday shows—and store window displays, whether they fall into the category of how-did-they-get-the-mechanical-chihuahua-dressed-as-Santa-Claus-to-play-the-trombone? or that of the live "psychiatrist" analyzing patients in the store's window. And spectacle means above all the sights and sounds of the heart of everything, New York's Fifth Avenue.

27

NEW YORK PUBLIC LIBRARY LION GETTING
HIS CHRISTMAS WREATH IN THE EARLY 1950s.

B. ALTMAN'S (northeast corner of 34th Street)—Just a few blocks east of Macy's, we begin with the first department store to move uptown from Ladies Mile to "middle" Fifth Avenue in 1913. Altman's, however, is now dead, having closed its doors in 1989. (The building recently reopened as the Science, Industry, and Business division of the New York Public Library.) Altman's had fancy Christmas window displays but for years no mannequins because Old Mr. Benjamin (as in "B.") Altman was offended by them. He was not alone. The Woman's Christian Temperance Union of New York City protested that it was indecent to dress "naked" mannequins in public when the windows were changed. Even in the 1930s, at least some of the imported male mannequins were extremely anatomically correct. They could be provided, it was said, with their external reproductive apparatus available in sizes "small," "medium," or "American." To avoid further offense to the WCTU, papers were thereafter put up in display windows when the mannequins were being "dressed," a practice that now serves to conceal surprise installations until they are ready to be sprung on the public.

The Christmas window displays that would spark a store's vital holiday retail sales became so elaborate by the 1960s that many large stores farmed out the actual execution of the displays to outside companies. The costs of these Christmas displays were—and are—guarded like new software operating formulae. However, the Chicago-based Silvestri company, that made some of the fanciest animated display work in the country, did a six-window display for Altman's of moving figures in 1960 for a cost of $70,000, unsurprising considering that to construct just two moving figures playing a chess game required animating them with 15 different internal motors.

EMPIRE STATE BUILDING (34th Street)—Diagonally southwest from the former Altman's, across the intersection of 34th and Fifth, is a Christmas display that one must gaze upward to see. In 1976, the Helmsley Company, managers of the Empire State Building, decided to light the landmark structure red, white, and blue for the bicentennial celebration, at the suggestion of advertising man Douglas Leigh. They then decided to expand the colored lighting for other holidays like Columbus Day, Easter and so forth—with red and green for Christmas. Years before Leigh had first thought of using different colored lights atop the Empire State Building to indicate what the weather would be. This was in the Depression, when the Empire State Building, like many New York skyscrapers, suffered from a lack of tenants. Leigh's idea was to have Coca-Cola become a prime tenant of the building, and then to put a key to the

THE EMPIRE STATE BUILDING, ITS UPPER FLOORS ILLLUMI-
NATED WITH RED AND GREEN LIGHTS AT CHRISTMAS.

Empire State Building colors on Coke bottles, so a Coke drinker could determine the weather. (Many years ago, Leigh, perhaps as a joke, told a reporter of his wish to turn the spire atop the Empire State Building into a 100-foot long cigarette with "smoke" coming out—and then illuminate it at night so it could be seen for 100 miles. But then it was Leigh who designed the famous giant Camel smoker that for years blew "smoke rings" of steam from his billboard out across Times Square.)

LORD & TAYLOR (38th Street)—"The store makes a great holiday display," said the *New York Tribune* admiringly back in 1874 when Mr. Samuel Lord and his wife's cousin, Mr. George Washington Taylor, had their store at 20th Street and Broadway. "Christmas trees, garlands of green, and bunting adorn the spaces of which Santa Claus is patron saint, while music and pleasant scents fill the air." In November 1937, some years after Lord & Taylor had moved to its present location, it delighted the holiday shopping public with a Christmas window that displayed *no* merchandise, a first in New York display window history. Instead, papier- mâché bells swung to and fro over a winter landscape. The ringing of the bells could be heard through an amplifier on Fifth Avenue; this transmission of music to those outside the store was also an innovation.

The "floors" of Lord & Taylor's display windows are mounted on hydraulic lifts which make it possible to decorate them at leisure out of sight of passersby. Even the main entrance on Fifth Avenue formerly rested on such a lift. When the store was closed each night, the entrance was lowered, decorated with a display, and then hoisted back into place to create another window—till the store opened again in the morning. Years ago the completion of the Christmas displays each year was celebrated with a party in the store's basement to which friends, reporters, and

MARY AND JOSEPH SEEK SHELTER UNDER THE BROOKLYN BRIDGE IN A 1955 LORD & TAYLOR DISPLAY WINDOW.

A WORKER AT SPAETH DESIGN PAINTS A ROCKING HORSE
DESTINED FOR A LORD & TAYLOR CHRISTMAS WINDOW.

others were directed by fancifully dressed mannequins over a floor spattered with gold paint for the occasion.

Since 1976, the Christmas window displays have been executed by Spaeth Design, which with a staff of some 100 people, many trained in theater design, develops its creations in 27,000 square feet on the first floor of an old industrial building between Ninth and Tenth Avenues on 55th Street. Started as an artificial foliage supplier by a former B. Altman employee, the company specializes in animated displays. It has customers all over the world, but regards the show windows it creates each Christmas for both Lord & Taylor and for Saks Fifth Avenue as its "showcases." Typically, the store's display director comes up with a concept within weeks after the most recent Christmas season, communicates it to Spaeth, and the Spaeth firm then builds the entire Christmas display at their plant in a period of six to eight months, with minor assembly required on site. Spaeth puts its real effort into the detailed recreation of setting and costumes rather than mechanical animation gadgetry, preferring, as the company's president David Spaeth puts it, not to compete with Disney in the simulated animation field. Nonetheless, the animated displays run on motors that are carefully designed to be independent of each other, so if one conks out the whole display doesn't shut down.

Lord & Taylor is one of the few survivors of the old Fifth Avenue which not so long ago was home to numerous chic department and "specialty" stores (as one item shops like shoe stores were called), e.g. Altman's and Bonwit Teller, before discount competitors, suburban shopping, and the creeping Warner Brothersization of the avenue took their toll.

NEW YORK PUBLIC LIBRARY (41st and 42nd Street)— The next bit of traditional holiday bedizening is at 41st Street, where the holiday pedestrian finds not a display window but

NEW YORK PUBLIC LIBRARY LION, 1996.

two awesome, holiday-wreathed kings of the jungle guarding the main entrance to the New York Public Library. "When I make a dog, I feel like a dog," said Edward Clark Potter, the dedicated animal sculptor who carved them back in 1911. (And "I suppose if I were to make a woman," he once said to his wife, "I suppose—it would look like a—horse!")

Potter worked diligently on the design of the library lions, even consulting a lion tamer. He put plaster models of the creatures outside on the steps, and when people complained that their manes were too hairy, he had them shaved down. Nicknamed by Mayor LaGuardia "Patience" (the northern one) and "Fortitude" (the southern) in the Thirties to denote the qualities New Yorkers would need to cope with the Depression, the lions got their first Christmas wreaths in 1950. Lights and big red bows were added the following year, and the beasts did splendidly until 1959, when vandals ignited the wreath around Patience's neck. The marble cracked, and wreathing was halted for two years, then reinstituted with fireproof intestines for the wreaths. Then one wreath was stolen—and so on. Now the lions wear great big wreaths six feet around that weigh about sixty pounds apiece.

CHRYSLER BUILDING (42nd Street and Lexington Avenue)—The ghost of Chrysler past. At 42nd Street look east for a moment after dark at the top of the Chrysler

Building. Try to imagine it not with the present genteel white outlines of lighting at the top but rather with large colored Christmas lights (some 500 of them) strung from the bottom of the spire fifteen stories down to the 58th floor where the gargoyles stare out—the lights spreading out just like a Christmas tree. So the building looked for a time during the holidays in the early 1960s. In 1963, it took six men thirty working days to install all the 60- to 400-watt bulbs on the steel cables necessary to create the "tree."

From here, a holiday stroll northward up Fifth Avenue naturally reaches a climax at about 51st Street, where topography and architecture conspire to produce a dramatic effect. Saks Fifth Avenue, with St. Patrick's Cathedral right next door, faces Rockefeller Center, creating a triangle that is a potent combination of religion, merchandizing, and quietly classy razzle-dazzle. The sense of having reached a high point has a physical as well as esthetic basis, because from 51st Street, Fifth Avenue slopes downwards in one direction to 59th Street and down to 44th Street in the other, so as you approach Saks and Rockefeller Center, you have a justifiable sense of having reached a "peak."

SAKS FIFTH AVENUE (51st Street)—If for years there was nothing terribly notable about Saks' windows at Christ-

SAKS FIFTH AVENUE, FESTOONED FOR CHRISTMAS.

mas, this may have been partly due to their relative inhospitability to elaborate displays. The Saks windows are not very deep, and the doors to them are narrow (30 inches) for the purpose of trying to squeeze display material through. Then, too, "Saks is in the glamour business," as one Saks display director put it rather loftily some years ago, "not the amusement business," a feeling which has changed only rather recently, as *all* business in America has become more entertainment-oriented.

Beginning in 1950, Saks *did* perch life-size papier-mâché carolers in niches above its street windows with organ pipes above them. The store then piped recorded music sung by the store's own employees' choir out to passersby. For a while in the Fifties, too, Saks had a Christmas "Stag Club," where men could go for advice on what to buy the women in their life. Saks was open only to men one night in the Christmas season so they could shop for the ladies, as the *Herald Tribune* put it, "protected from the hordes of daytime shoppers"—and provided with a free bar.

The Saks Christmas window displays that the Spaeths have made for the store since 1977 are designed not only for that particular year's holiday season in New York but to travel for succeeding Christmases to one of the many other Saks stores around the country, a logical, if unromantic, way of amortizing the displays' considerable cost.

ROCKEFELLER CENTER (48th-51st Streets)—The spectator who turns directly around from the window display at Saks will be looking at Rockefeller Center on the other side of Fifth Avenue. After crossing the avenue, he or she will be standing at the top of a long, gently sloping promenade looking down through Rockefeller Center's Channel Gardens at its famous Christmas tree. Since 1954 the promenade has been accented at Christmas by twelve 9-foot-high angels made from aluminum and copper wire that point their trumpets towards the tree. Dreamed up by Robert Carson, an architect at the Center who directed

VALERIE CLAREBOUT
AND ONE OF HER ANGELS.

its Christmas decorations, they are the handiwork of Valerie Clarebout, an Englishwoman who came to America in the early 1950s after study at the Royal Academy of Art, worked for a display corporation in New York and one day found herself $10 short of the $35 she needed to buy a dachshund she wanted. So she went to the Rockefeller Center people and made them a two-foot-high model of an angel. Before long they asked her for a dozen—full-size. Since her death in 1982 the angels have been maintained and set up each year by the ubiquitous Spaeths, for whom the celestial creatures pose exasperating problems of handling. Even the slightest touch of the light-weight aluminum will alter their shapes, and, of course, when their shapes change, their paint job flakes off, too.

THE TREE (Rockefeller Center)—The first Rockefeller Center Christmas tree, a mere twelve or so feet tall, was put up by workmen in 1931 at the rubble-strewn site of the innumerable speakeasies on and around 50th Street which were torn down to make way for the new skyscraper complex. Needing all the money they could get in those desperate Depression years, the men worked late Christmas Eve and were paid their wages in front of the tree, which they had decorated with some tinsel, paper, and a tin can or two.

In 1933 the Rockefeller Center management took over the Christmas tree idea. The first "official" Rockefeller Center tree, a definite change from the scraggly Yuletide creation that the workmen had erected, had seven hundred blue and white lights on it and was set up on the sidewalk in front of the then-new RCA (now GE) building.

WORKMEN AT ROCKEFELLER CENTER
WITH ITS FIRST CHRISTMAS TREE, 1931.

The Rockefeller Center tree was not the first large outdoor community Christmas tree in Manhattan. Beginning in 1912, a "Tree of Light" had been erected with singing and band music each Christmas in Madison Square Park. The *Times* called the Madison Square Park tree "the skyscraper tree that stands 63 feet in its socks, as it were." And, just like the Rockefeller Center tree, it stood in

THE MADISON SQUARE PARK TREE, PRECURSOR
OF THE ROCKFELLER CENTER TREE.

front of a giant skyscraper, the Metropolitan Life Insurance tower overlooking Madison Square Park, which in 1912 was the tallest building in the world. The idea of an outdoor Christmas tree was then so novel that lots of people thought the Madison Square tree must be going up *in*doors, inside Madison Square Garden, which was then located, logically enough, at the corner of Madison Square Park. And so an avalanche of letters poured in asking for tickets. But no. The idea was for it to be, as the *Times* said, a "People's Tree," for rich and poor alike to look at.

Other outdoor trees followed. In 1926, the New York Electrical League put up a 35-foot-high Christmas tree in Times Square bearing 3,500 colored lights and blaring Christmas carols through amplifiers. By then Wall Streeters had begun setting up a tree each year on Broad Street, and the Park Avenue Baptist Church put up a big tree with lights on it that were lit from dusk till midnight.

For Rockefeller Center, making a big deal out of an outdoor Christmas tree was a shrewd move. The giant new RCA building that towered over the tree and was the core of Rockefeller Center opened in 1933 at the height of the Depression. As a result, like every other skyscraper in the city, it desperately needed tenants. Indeed, the Center's management sought them so avidly that in 1934 Rockefeller Center was sued by another skyscraper owner for allegedly stealing his tenants. Attention-getting devices like a dramatic outdoor Christmas tree could do no harm in such an economic climate.

For several years the Rockefeller Center tree was put up in the sunken plaza where the skating rink now is because the plaza was not effectively drawing shoppers down to the below-ground shops in the Center as it was supposed to. (The skating rink, a last-ditch effort to find *some* use for the plaza, was first opened on Christmas Day, 1936.) For years the same Robert Carson who commissioned Valerie Clarebout's angels for the Channel Gardens did the designs for the tree's decorations. Blue lights only were used to decorate the tree in 1938, and floodlights in 1939. In 1941 plans called for putting a candle in every window of the seventy-story RCA building. However, the plan was dropped after Pearl Harbor because it would have taken an impossibly long time to douse so many lights in the building during an air raid blackout. Ornaments but no tree lights were used to decorate the tree during the remainder of World War II. In 1945, 700 ten-inch fluorescent ornaments were suspended from the tree and illuminated with beams of ultraviolet light, and in 1949 the tree was sprayed silver. In 1973, because of the energy crisis, the evergreen was decorated with tiny bulbs with reflectors rather than big lights.

THE ROCKEFELLER CENTER TREE IN 1996
WITH PROMETHEUS.

The ornaments are no more, however, because big sky-scrapers like the RCA building can create a wind tunnel effect that tends to send everything not nailed down hurtling along adjacent streets. Some decades ago, for example, the decorators thought it would be nice to have long aluminum icicles hanging from the tree. The wind came up, and the icicles, not that well secured, "flew around the area like spears," observed a Center bigwig thoughtfully. (No one was hit.) Likewise, when little plastic discs were used as decorations one year, the wind sent miniature flying saucers all over the place; a Center employee found one down on 42nd Street. So nowadays there are lights and *just* lights, though some 25,000 of them—and *no* decorations, except for the star atop the tree, a sixty-pound beauty, four-and-a-half feet tall and bearing five 150-watt bulbs.

The tree itself generally has to be chosen by mid-summer at the latest to allow enough time to work out its transportation, erection, and decoration. Rockefeller Center director of horticulture David Murbach whisks about in a helicopter at an altitude of 900 feet over the landscape to try to locate likely specimens. Typically, the ideal tree is not from a forest, because Norway spruce, the favored variety, is not a native tree. Also, a tree's branches do not get enough room in the woods to acquire the majesty necessary to grace Rockefeller Center. ("I always envision these trees as having a certain feeling, a certain carriage, posture," Murbach has said, "a sense of character that seems noble—like Katharine Hepburn.") A chosen tree's owners often part with it fairly willingly, not just because of the publicity but because trees that have grown to seventy or eighty feet, the optimum height, are typically overwhelming a property's sunlight, looming over its owner's house, and are getting so old that they are not long for this world anyway.

For the last fifteen years, the tree has been cut down, hauled to the city and set up at Rockefeller Center by the Torsilieri family, who run a landscaping business in Gladstone, New Jersey. The tree is transported in a special trailer that can accommodate up to a 100-foot-long tree. The evergreen customarily weighs in at three tons or more and is anchored to various parts of the skating rink and the GE Building with huge wires by a crew of some 15 to 20 men with a crane. Trimming is done with a scaffold made of some two-and-a-half miles' worth of wood since a workman fell in 1951 and broke his leg while trimming without one.

"From the business sense, it's what distinguishes Rockefeller Center from its competition," said the director of marketing communications somewhat awkwardly about the tree some years ago. If one were cynical one might suspect that such distinction has perhaps been useful in marketing an aging office building that must compete with newer structures built for the fax and computer age.

As one struggles through the crowds to try to get a close-up glimpse of the tree, it becomes evident that it is a very, very popular tourist attraction. In 1996 the crush at the tree—some 500,000 visitors each weekend after it was lit—obliged Rockefeller Center for the first time to institute strict crowd control measures. One was permitted only a one-way walk *down* the Channel Gardens and around the skating rink in a westerly and then southerly direction to see the tree.

But then New York at Christmas is increasingly becoming a madhouse. "More people come to New York City to enjoy Christmas, to enjoy the holidays, than anyplace else in the United States," said Mayor Rudolph Giuliani in 1996. Hotel occupancy rates in the city soared that same year to an astronomical 85% (they were less than 70% in the early 1990s), and in fact the Plaza Hotel contacts favored guests as early as August to remind them to book for the holidays. Broadway theaters do more business Christmas week—$14 million in 1996, from 239,296 patrons—than during any other week in the year. The number of cars entering Manhattan each day, normally 980,000, jumps by 75,000 to 100,000 during the weeks before Christmas. These days of horrendous traffic are known as "gridlock days," and the city generally declares 11 to 12 of them in the month between Thanksgiving and New Year's, the day after Thanksgiving usually being *the* worst traffic day of the year.

And what might this mean to *you*? In the area around Rockefeller Center buses trying to get across town crawl at an average of only two miles per hour (humans walk at about three miles per hour), which, of course, is why God invented feet and the subway.

THE INTERIOR OF ST. PATRICK'S CATHEDRAL.

CHESTNUTS ROAST ON THE OPEN FIRE
OF THIS MIDTOWN VENDOR.

ST. PATRICK'S CATHEDRAL (50th Street)—Speaking of crowds, one of the most popular Christmas Eve services in Manhattan is the midnight mass traditionally celebrated at St. Patrick's. In fact, those wishing to attend must obtain tickets in advance (the cathedral holds only about 2,500); although the service is also televised.

Somewhere along in this vicinity you are likely to catch a whiff of the robust, smoky odor emanating from the wares of the hot chestnut vendor, one of the infallible olfactory indicators that Christmas is near. Street vendors find chestnuts a tricky food—they don't sell well enough to be an item all by themselves. Also, unlike other cold weather favorites such as hot dogs and pretzels, chestnuts dry up after an hour's roasting, so they must be sold quickly. Time was when the city's major chestnut distributor daily popped out ten or twenty 55-pound bags of the goodies, which are imported from Italy since the blight that decimated American chestnut trees early in this century. Recently, due to city regulation of street vendors, bag distribution is down to about ten a week at most.

CARTIER'S (52nd Street)—In a costless gift to passersby, Cartier's in the early Eighties started wrapping its store in a giant (ninety feet by fifty feet) red sailcloth ribbon and bow that takes roughly three days to maneuver into place. If the weather is good, that is. Arranging the cloth is all but impossible in strong winds or on rainy days when the sailcloth gets waterlogged. In 1994, Santa ceremonially put the finishing touches on the Cartier bow from a cherry picker, and in 1995 "elves" climbed the building under Santa's direction to put on the finishing touches. (In 1996, the elves just handed out hot chocolate.)

Cartier's made an unusual offer during the 1996 Christmas season at the height of the "Tickle-Me-Elmo" (remember?) toy craze. It put one of the then virtually unobtainable toys in a window and offered the toy free—

"ELF" CLIMBING CARTIER'S IN 1995 EN ROUTE TO TOUCH UP THE BRIGHT RED RIBBON "TIED" AROUND THE BUILDING.

CARTIER'S, IN ALL ITS CHRISTMAS GLORY.

to whoever paid $1 million for the diamond necklace draped around its neck.

TRUMP TOWER (56th Street)—On the setbacks above the southwest corner of the building miniature Christmas trees are arranged during the holiday season and the building's somewhat garish interior is decorated to beat the band. Trump Tower replaced the fashionable women's store Bonwit Teller, which, like Saks, once helped bewildered men to shop for their women at Christmas. "We'd serve champagne, models would wander around in 'at-home wear,' as we called it," a former employee remembered of the Sixties. "And we would help the guys pick out gifts for their wives or mistresses." Bonwit's also struck an early blow for feminism by having a *Mrs*. Santa Claus in 1965— an actress in old-fashioned cap, gray wig, and rimless specs—instead of the old bearded gentleman.

In 1955, Bonwit Teller head Walter Hoving rescued the store next door from destruction, a lucky thing for passersby, Audrey Hepburn, and everyone else, for the store was...

TIFFANY & CO. (57th Street)—The best place in New York for breakfast, of course. The window displays at Tiffany's must fit into tiny spaces (five windows all measuring 36 inches high by 22 inches deep), as befits windows whose purpose is to show off jewelry. For many years these displays, including the two into which Audrey Hepburn gazes during the opening credits of *Breakfast at Tiffany's*, were the work of Gene Moore. A thin, intense native of Birmingham, Alabama, he had originally wanted to be a painter. The imperious Walter Hoving brought Moore in from Bonwit's as part of a plan to make Tiffany's less stuffy and more chic. Moore created a series of studiedly sly, elegant tableaux in the tiny windows: a Santa fishing in a dyed lake (of paraffin) for a bit of emerald; a woman being rescued by a Saint Bernard bearing a bottle of champagne instead of brandy (her hand, thrusting through the snow, imploringly reached out a champagne glass); and so on. Moore employed such "assistants" on his Bonwit's and Tiffany's windows as artists Jasper Johns, Robert Rauschenberg, James Rosenquist, and Andy Warhol.

But then at its height the New York store display window, like other forms of commercial design in Manhattan, was the product of a cross-pollenation between the fine and applied arts. Moore himself did sets and costumes for the dance company of his friend Paul Taylor and for a London production of John Gielgud, who called him up out of the blue after seeing some of his windows. Tom Lee, who did Bonwit Teller's and Bergdorf Goodman's windows and

A 1996 CHRISTMAS WINDOW AT TIFFANY'S.

got his start at Macy's, designed sets and costumes for an Irving Berlin musical and for Lincoln Kirstein's American Ballet. He also did shows for the Metropolitan Museum— and he designed the Dove soap bar. Norman Bel Geddes, a window designer at Macy's and Franklin Simon, did many set and costume designs for the Metropolitan Opera, in addition to designing everything from vacuum cleaners to cars. And Albert Bliss, longtime Macy's window display artificer and a supplier of figures for Lord & Taylor's windows, was a one-time child actor who later studied under Ashcan School painters John Sloan and Robert Henri and at the Bauhaus.

Today Moore's hand-picked successor (Moore retired in 1995) follows in his minimalist tradition. Woody Shimko stepped out into the master's trail with a 1995 Christmas window featuring miniature birds playing the organ, singing gospel, and carrying on in Times Square on New Year's.

SNOWFLAKE (over the intersection of Fifth Avenue and 57th Street)—In 1984 Tiffany's took the lead in hiring the same Douglas Leigh who had eight years before devised the lighting for the Empire State Building to design a $60,000 snowflake some two-and-a-half stories high consisting of 6,000 light bulbs. Anchored each holiday season to corners of the Warner Brothers, Bergdorf Goodman, Tiffany, and Crown

**ᗑOUGLAS LEIGH, THE MAN
BEHIND THE SNOWFLAKE,
AS WELL AS THE EMPIRE
STATE BUILDING LIGHTS.**

buildings, it hangs over the intersection of Fifth Avenue and 57th Street. Leigh, incidentally, is also responsible for designing the external illumination of the Crown Building, as well as that of the Con Edison Building, Park Avenue's Helmsley Building, and the Citicorp Building.

It is nice to *see* a snowflake in an era when Christmas seems increasingly to be a time of warm drizzling rain. Actually, though, since 1912, there have been only fourteen "white Christmases" in New York City, if you mean a Christmas with at least an inch of snow on the ground, and only *one*, if you mean Christmas Days since that year on which at least an inch of snow actually *fell*. (Although the city's biggest recorded snowfall hit on December 26, 1947, dumping 26.4 inches of the white stuff in Central Park within 24 hours.)

ᗑ Fifth Avenue time-out: West down 57th Street just beyond the intersection of Sixth Avenue there is an imposing structure at 109 West 57th Street, namely, Steinway Hall (the ground floor is still a showroom for the celebrated

THE SNOWFLAKE AT THE INTERSECTION OF 57TH STREET
AND FIFTH AVENUE.

Steinway pianos). It was here that Dylan Thomas recorded his famous story, "A Child's Christmas in Wales," and thereby hangs a tale. Marianne Roney and Barbara Cohen, both Hunter College Class of '50, had been students, *inter alia*, of Greek, Sanskrit, Old German, and Old French. Even while working at such dreary jobs as writing record album notes, the two young graduates cherished the dream of one day recording the great poets of the era. Then they heard that Dylan Thomas was in town. They went in December 1951 to hear him read at the 92nd Street YMHA Poetry Center and sent up a note with their names (but only with the *initials* of their first names—so they would sound like important *men*.) The result was disappointing. After five days of phone calls, however, they got through to Thomas at the Hotel Chelsea where he was staying. The poet and the women then went to lunch at the hotel's restaurant where they asked him to record for them. He agreed, even though in their naïveté the women let Thomas pay for the lunch. When he could only think of a few poems to read they warned him too much space would be left on the then standard 33 1/3 rpm long playing record. After a moment, he recalled "a little story I wrote. In a magazine—was it *Harper's Bazaar*? Not a very long story. But I can't think what the name was… something about Christmas, a Christmas in Wales…" Indeed, Thomas had originally written "A Child's Christmas in Wales" as a short piece for the magazine. So a copy of *Harper's Bazaar* was dredged up. Thomas then read the piece at Steinway Hall "for the recording, in that surging, passionate, forlorn voice of his, equally bereft of self-pity and of hope," Barbara Cohen later recalled. The tale of the little boy and the Welsh Christmas went on to become a mainstay of Roney and Cohen's enterprise, which they named Caedmon records, and thereafter their spoken literature recordings of everyone from Thomas Mann to Auden grew rapidly.

BERGDORF GOODMAN (57th Street)—Traditionally an adult-oriented women's fashion store, in 1996 Bergdorf

A FAIRY TALE WINDOW AT BERGDORF GOODMAN.

made a stab at the Christmas kiddie trade, with a series of somewhat dark, modish windows of fairy tales (e.g. Snow White in a Heidi Weisel dress and jacket). They had *edge*.

The one featuring Puss in Boots, for example, had in Puss' place only boots—the fabled cat having presumably disappeared.

F.A.O. SCHWARZ (58th Street)—And so to our last stop on Fifth Avenue. Frederick Augustus Otto Schwarz was the son of a Westphalian goldsmith

F.A.O. (FREDERICK AUGUSTUS OTTO) SCHWARZ— THE ORIGINAL.

notable chiefly for making a gold bathtub for Napoleon's brother. F.A.O. came to the United States with *his* brothers in the 1850s. It was then customary for German manufacturers to send unsolicited sample products through the mail to America in order to drum up business. Some toys dispatched in this fashion arrived in 1862 in a shipment of stationery at Schwerdtmann's stationery store in Baltimore where the Schwarzes were employed. Frederick and his brothers found that the toys outsold the stationery. Brother Henry therefore opened up a toy store in Baltimore (he

FORMER F.A.O. SCHWARZ EMPLOYEE MAURICE SENDAK'S
WINDOW DISPLAY FOR SONY, 1996.

was supposedly the first ever to employ a live Santa in his store), and his brothers followed suit in other cities. Frederick took New York, where in 1870 he opened the Schwarz Toy Bazaar at 765 Broadway, whose aptly decorous motto was: "To offer the best goods, at most reasonable prices, with polite attention."

At first, F.A.O. catered only to New York's carriage trade. At one time, indeed, Schwarz didn't even put prices on its wares. The store sold toys often not available anywhere else in America, in an era when most toys sold in the United States were still imports. Each year the jolly, white-bearded Schwarz, who delighted in his resemblance to Santa Claus, journeyed early in the season to Europe, where he visited toymakers, asking, "What can you do for me?"—meaning, can you make a distinctive toy for me? Other toy dealers making the rounds in his wake soon found they were too late on their journey to Paris, Switzerland, or Nuremberg (the latter then best known as a city of premier toymakers), to get the best toys.

The Depression hit even Social Register customers, however. So Schwarz began to stock toys that other stores carried and to seek other patrons in addition to the wealthy. Along came Joshua Lionel Cowen, a native New Yorker who carved his first wooden train at age eight, almost blew up his parents' kitchen with his experimenting, and with one assistant began manufacturing miniature electric trains in 1900 in a loft on Cortlandt Street. Schwarz became Cowen's biggest retail customer. The store displayed the Lionel trains, since Mr. Cowen had given the toys his middle name, on its second floor for many Christmases. There they ran along miles of track, smoke pouring out of their tiny smokestacks, with miniature whistles sounding periodically, to the fascination of countless New Yorkers young and old. (Lionel, with medical advice, carefully designed the smoke pellets and other train accessories to be non-toxic if ingested by small humans.)

Notwithstanding Lionel's popularity with the masses, Schwarz was still known for its slightly lofty cachet before it was taken over by *Parents Magazine* in 1963. When Schwarz had finally put prices on its toys, it was, typically, in code that kids couldn't read. To each of the various ten letters that form the German word "borgenicht" ("don't borrow"), a corresponding number was assigned; the appropriate letters for a given price were then inscribed on the tag placed on the toy.

Talent and imagination were never in short supply at the old store. Sales counters at F.A.O. Schwarz were built child rather than adult height, and when in 1948 two brothers named Sendak approached Schwarz with some elaborate wooden toys they had made, the store was so impressed that it hired the twenty-year-old Maurice as an assistant window display man. He held the job for three years. In fact, Maurice became fascinated with the children's books illustrated by Walter Crane, George Cruikshank, and Randolph Caldecott in the store's book department. The store's book buyer finally introduced him to an editor at Harper and Brothers—and the rest, as they say, is history. In 1996 Sendak came full circle when he designed a set of six animated windows for the Sony building on Madison Avenue and 55th Street based on his book, *Where the Wild Things Are*. Those ferocious dream creatures in a *New York* Christmas? "New York," said Sendak, "is full of wild things."

The fact of the store's German ownership almost bankrupted it in World War I when there were rumors that Schwarz was giving money to Kaiser Wilhelm and harboring spies. Likewise, during World War II Mrs. Irving Berlin heard at a cocktail party that Hitler's portrait hung in the executive offices and had to be given a tour to unconvince her. Today F.A.O. Schwarz is owned by a Dutch conglomerate. It is expanding rapidly to meet the threat (around the corner and internationally) from toy purveyors like Warner Brothers and Disney that have enormous brand name recognition and extensive advertising outlets at their disposal. In the process, Schwarz is reverting to the store's old policy of carrying largely products that no other store offers. In 1996, three-quarters of the toys it sold were not available at other retailers. And once again it caters to the rich and famous—it has closed the store for Michael Jackson to do his shopping there.

THE SALVATION ARMY
FREE
CHRISTMAS
DINNER
TO 25,000 POOR
OF THIS CITY.

"KEEP THE POT BOILING."

$\mathcal{T}$HE $\mathcal{S}$IDEWALKS OF $\mathcal{N}$EW $\mathcal{Y}$ORK

$\mathbf{A}$mid all the glitter of some of the larger avenues and streets, it is easy to forget that at the foot of the giant buildings of Manhattan, away from the glamorous windows of Fifth Avenue, there are other aspects of the true New York Christmas. The Christmas tree tradition was German in origin, and in the 1830s New Yorkers already were venturing across the East River to the (then separate) municipality of Brooklyn to view that city's Teutonic population's "custom of dressing a 'Christmas Tree.'" In 1851 one Mark Carr, a Catskills logger, erected the first Christmas tree stand in Man-

69

hattan at Washington Market, the city's produce center, which was located near where the World Trade Center is now. He paid $1 for rental of the sidewalk space. By the early 1880s, an estimated 200,000 Christmas trees were said to be sold in the city annually, most of them coming from Maine by railroad or steamer.

The law currently provides that anyone may sell trees in the month of December on the sidewalk without a vendor's license, which opens up the business to casual sellers. But a seller must have the permission of the owners of the building in front of which he or she sets up, which frequently means a gratuity changing hands. Also, at least in theory, the vendor is supposed to leave a nine-and-a-half-foot wide pedestrian walkway on the sidewalk. Nowadays, the trees sold are largely firs because they don't tend to turn yellow as do pines, which are also harder to clip into shape and less straight than firs. Perhaps only some 10% of the trees sold by sidewalk vendors come from New York State. The rest are from as far afield as Oregon, Wisconsin, Quebec, Nova Scotia, and the Carolinas. Before the mid 1960s, most Christmas trees sold in the city came from natural forests. They were not mass grown on level farmland with their tops pruned off as today's trees are and therefore were thinner and more conical than today's squatter, denser-branched trees.

At one time the fire laws prohibited any trees indoors. In those pre-electric days the trees were particularly flammable because they were lit with candles. Then in 1882 Thomas Edison set up the world's first functioning electrical distribution system from his Pearl Street station in the Wall Street area. Edison Electric company vice-president Edward Johnson had the bright idea of getting the Edison lab to make up special wired bulbs for him to use on his Christmas tree. From there the idea spread, and today Christmas trees inside apartments are legal.

However, there is still a city ban on live Christmas trees in other indoor locations. Under Local Law 29, there can be no live or recently cut tree (though fireproofed wreaths are okay) in any apartment lobbies, office building vestibules, or other similar space in a building occupied by seventy-five or more people. Which is why so much of the indoor Christmas greenery in public places in New York City is phony.

And *what* happens after the holidays to all those Christmas trees in the city that are *real* (by the estimate of the New York Christmas Tree Growers Association, some 1.5 million)? In the bad old days trees were burned and used as landfill in various dumps around the city. In 1960, Sanitation Commissioner Paul Screvane grimly warned that by 1980 there would be nowhere left in the city to bury the trees. So in 1973 the city started a tree recycling plant in Washington Square Park. The trunks were cut up and made into paper products by a paper company, and everything else was pulverized and used for mulch in city parks. Nowadays trees left out on the curb in early January are collected by the Sanitation Department. The trees—some 1,670 tons' worth in January 1997—are then turned into mulch, mixed with compost, and made available to individual gardeners and local garden groups in the city, with a small amount being spread in city parks.

The Rockefeller Center tree is a special case. Beginning around 1940, there was public concern about simply throwing away the Rockefeller Center trees after the holidays. So they were re-planted after use. Nowadays, the Rockefeller Center tree trunk is cut into sections which are used by the U.S. Equestrian Team for jump training, and the rest of the tree is turned into mulch for parks.

Speaking of sidewalks, what of those ringing bells and pleas to help the needy on the sidewalks from the uniformed prickers of our conscience at Christmastime? As Shaw's *Major Barbara* reminds us, the Salvation Army was British in origin, the brainchild of "General" William Booth. After the organization was exported to America, the first Salvation Army kettles began appearing on the streets of New York around 1890. The custom of ringing

In 1996 FEMALE SIDEWALK SANTAS GOT A
SPECIAL DONNA KARAN OUTFIT.

bells over kettles originated in San Francisco a few years before with the slogan, "Help keep the pot boiling." (The kettle was a symbol of the good Christmas dinners for the poor which the Army sought to provide.) In its early days, a not-atypical Manhattan Christmas found the Army feeding 4,000 people and distributing another 4,000 baskets containing enough for a family of five, i.e. a chicken, a can of soup, potatoes, plum pudding, apples, tea, coffee, and two loaves of bread.

Today the money goes for the Army's various social service programs. A combination of its officers, cadets (who are officer trainees), paid kettle workers, and volunteers collects half to three-quarters of a million dollars from its approximately 100 New York City kettles. These are generally set up the day after Thanksgiving and taken down the day before Christmas. And by tradition, the Army's musicians play in the 21 Club each year.

In 1896 General Booth's son broke with his father and the Salvation Army and founded the Volunteers of America. Instead of using uniformed officers and kettles, the Volunteers since 1903 have manned the sidewalks of New York with chimneys and bell-ringing "Sidewalk Santas." They collect money that goes towards food vouchers for needy families. 1996's thirty Manhattan Santas included volunteers (twelve students from Baruch College among them), as well as indigent and recovering men and women from the Volunteers' shelters or elsewhere who earn a modest stipend in return for their bell-ringing. The bell-ringing follows a brief training (sample guidance: "Eating garlic prior to assuming your chimney post may drive down revenues for the day"). 1995 saw the first female Sidewalk Santa in New York; in 1996 there were fifteen. A member of the board of directors of the Volunteers contacted Donna Karan, asking if she could devise a costume more appropriate for female Santas, and her DKNY obligingly designed a snappy-looking outfit consisting of a red down jacket, black turtleneck, black ski pants, white gloves and belt, and a Santa hat.

$\mathcal{S}$ANTOLOGY

I t is appropriate that the streets of Manhattan are filled with Santas at Christmastime since Santa Claus was invented in New York City.

In 1822, Clement Moore, the distinguished professor of Hebrew and Greek at the General Theological Seminary, lived with his 75-year-old mother, his wife and his children, Margaret, Charity, Ben, Mary, Clement, and Emily, in a mansion in suburban greenery outside the limits of developed Manhattan and beyond its street lamps on what is now 23rd Street in Chelsea. For the Christmas holiday that year, he com-

$\mathcal{V}$IRGINIA O'HANLON, WHOSE LETTER AS A
LITTLE GIRL PROMPTED THE LEGENDARY REPLY,
"YES, VIRGINIA, THERE IS A SANTA CLAUS..."

posed a little poem to amuse his young. It was called "A Visit from St. Nicholas," or, as it is more popularly known today, "'Twas The Night Before Christmas," and Moore recited it at the family Christmas. The poem blended a host of elements familiar to Moore personally or through reading, including the physique and physiognomy of the red-faced and portly Dutchman in Moore's neighborhood who

CLEMENT MOORE

served as the physical model for his gift-bearing Saint Nicholas.

St. Nicholas, the bishop of Myrna in the fourth century, was the most popular saint in pre-Reformation times, the patron saint, *inter alia*, of pawnbrokers, children, mariners, and those who had been unfairly deprived of victory in law suits. Then, in his satirical 1809 *History of New York*, Washington Irving, who was, incidentally, the brother of Moore's classmate at Columbia College, Peter Irving, fancifully suggested that St. Nicholas was a patron saint of old Dutch New Amsterdam. Irving described St. Nicholas traveling through the skies of the New World in an air-borne wagon and horse to deliver holiday gifts to well-behaved children. For his Christmas verse, Moore borrowed heavily from Irving; the phrase "laying a finger aside of his nose" Moore took for his poem almost word for word from Irving's book. However, Moore made Irving's horse and wagon into reindeer and a sleigh, the sleigh being a standard means of New York winter street transportation in those long ago days.

The portly St. Nicholas acquired a new name. By 1830 Manhattanite B. G. Jansen was advertising a shop devoted to *"Santaclaus"* that offered a "very extensive assortment of Bibles, Prayer Books, Psalm Books, Hymn Books, Toys

'Twas the night before Christmas, when all through
   the house
Not a creature was stirring, not even a mouse;
The stockings were hung by the chimney with care,
In hopes that St. Nicholas soon would be there;
The children were nestled all snug in their beds;
While visions of sugar-plums danced in their heads;
And mamma in her 'kerchief, and I in my cap,
Had just settled our brains for a long winter's nap;
When out on the lawn there arose such a clatter,
I sprang from the bed to see what what was the matter.
Away to the window I flew like a flash,
Tore open the shutters and threw up the sash.
The moon, on the breast of the new-fallen snow,

THE OPENING LINES OF "'TWAS THE THE NIGHT BEFORE CHRISTMAS" IN CLEMENT MOORE'S OWN HANDWRITING.

and ChapBooks," in his capacity as "Agent of St. Nicholas." Two years later, an observer of Christmas Eve in New York noted that "whole rows of confectionery stores and toy stores, fancifully, and often splendidly, decorated with festoons of bright silk drapery, interspersed with flowers and evergreens, are brilliantly illuminated with gas-lights, arranged in every shape and figure that fancy can devise. During the evening, until midnight, these places are crowded with visiters of both sexes and all ages; some selecting toys and fruits for holyday presents; others merely lounging from shop to shop to enjoy the varied scene."

It was left to New York illustrator and cartoonist Thomas Nast (who came up with the donkey and elephant as symbols for the Democrats and the Republicans) to expand Santa in the 1860s from the "elf" Moore had made him into today's full-size and unequivocally benevolent Santa. An illustrator for *Harper's Weekly*, Nast also located Santa's headquarters at the North Pole, gave him his costume of a wide belt and ermine-trimmed red tunic and pants (retaining the red garb of the bishop that the real Saint Nicholas had been), and dreamed up the book in which Santa wrote down a list of what presents children wanted.

New York City also dealt firmly and famously with skepticism about Santa, too.

One day in 1897 a letter made its way to the editorial offices of the *New York Sun*:

DEAR EDITOR:

I am eight years old.

Some of my little friends say there is no Santa Claus.

Papa says "If you see it in the Sun *it's so."*

Please tell me the truth, is there a Santa Claus?

VIRGINIA O'HANLON

115 West Ninety-fifth Street

The *Sun* was a paper cheerfully dedicated to purveying all sorts of foolishness to its readers if the occasion called for it. As Edward Mitchell, the editorial page chief who received little Virginia's letter, once told a Columbia Journalism School class, many newspaper readers are deeply preoccupied with questions "such as 'How Should Engaged Couples Act at the Circus?' or 'What Is a Dodunk?' or 'Do the Angels Play Football?'"

Unsurprisingly, then, Mitchell handed Virginia's communication to Francis Pharcellus Church, a rather sardonic former Civil War correspondent for the *New York Times*, and told him to draft a reply to the little girl's letter. Church "bristled and pooh-poohed at the subject," but went off "with an air of resignation to his desk," Mitchell recalled.

Church wrote Virginia a reply. "IS THERE A SANTA CLAUS?" appeared in the September 21, 1897 *Sun*. Certainly there was. "Virginia," it said, "your little friends are wrong. They have been affected by the skepticism of a skeptical age. They do not believe except they see. Yes, Virginia," said Church, "there is a Santa Claus. He exists as certainly as love and generosity and devotion exist..." And so on.

The phrase, "Yes, Virginia..." passed into the language. Virginia herself, it is pleasing to note, grew up to get a B.A. from Hunter College in 1910, an M.A. from Columbia, and then a Fordham doctorate. She taught in the New York City public school system until her retirement in 1959, rising to become principal of P.S. 401 in Brooklyn, and dying in 1971. (A happy contrast to at least two of Clement Moore's grown children, whom a contemporary found at their maturity to manifest "a compound of imbecility deep beyond all fathom with an appetite for chambermaids beyond all precedent.")

Did Virginia ever get to *meet* Santa, though?

Well, as early as 1888 the New York store of J. Lichtenstein & Sons was inviting New York youngsters "to come and see a real live Santa Claus." He was, as other Santas were to be through the years, ensconced in a grotto. It was not long before Macy's had a Santa, too, as did the other department stores. Indeed, the giant Wanamaker's between 9th and 10th Streets on Broadway (an offshoot of the Philadelphia store) held a parade inside the store in 1919 complete with Santa on a palanquin carried by four Eskimoes, a uniformed brass band, children dressed as stars and snowflakes, a gang of children's book characters and so on. (Wanamaker's also had the dubious distinction of pioneering the use of an in-store telephone in its toy department to call Santa.) Gimbel's at one point had eight live reindeer (i.e., Donder, Blitzen, etc.) in their store in Herald Square. For a number of years the Gimbel's window displayed a chimney out of which a live Santa popped every fifteen minutes or so to talk through a microphone to the goggle-eyed kids looking in from the street outside. Gimbel's Santa could be persuaded, with little difficulty, to sing an unsubtle ditty, which, to the tune of "Jingle Bells," went, "Gimbel bells, Gimbel bells, ringing in the air / We have the very gayest toys since Greeley crossed the Square."

And did it pay off? One New York reporter in the early part of the century described how at an unnamed department store Santa and the store's manager began each day with a review of the items that were not selling. Later that day, as the children were hoisted onto Santa's lap, Santa would mentally consult his list of slow-moving items. "What about a nice desk for Christmas?" he would ho-ho-

ho. "Santa thinks you would love a desk that has two special drawers, a handy roll-away top…." Today, no one would be quite so crass, perhaps—or optimistic. The store Santa pays off in good will, not readily countable dollars.

The single most celebrated helper Santa has ever had began life as a department store creation, namely, Ruldolph the red-nosed you-know-what. Rudolph's story was actually a 1939 promotional booklet distributed by the Montgomery Ward department store in Chicago. Johnny Marks, a former Paris music student and nightclub piano player, saw the booklet and wrote the title down in a notebook. Then he went off to war, where he won four battle stars and a Bronze Star for playing a major role in capturing 100 German soldiers.

Perhaps because so many people were writing Christmas songs after the war, Marks tried to make a song out of Rudolph—but he couldn't get it quite right. And then one day while walking along a Greenwich Village street it hit him—his melody for the "red-nosed reindeer" part made the note to which "-nosed" was sung a low note—but the melody, he realized, should instead go *up* on "-nosed."

Bingo!

Marks sent the completed song to a whole bunch of people, including Bing Crosby and Dinah Shore, adding as an afterthought cowboy singer Gene Autry. None showed any interest. But Autry's wife liked the song so Autry decided to record it on a record as a filler. Came the annual Gene Autry rodeo at the old Madison Square Garden on 50th Street and Eighth Avenue in 1949, and Autry sang the song for the first time. "We had a guy dressed in a reindeer costume with a big bulb of a nose, and when I got to the second verse of the song they threw a blue light on him and he danced," Autry recalled some thirty years later. "We did a class act."

Johnny Marks was inspired to create other Christmas melodies—notably, "Rockin' Around the Christmas Tree" and "A Holly, Jolly Christmas." But "that music for Rudolph is one of the great all-time melodies," Marks once modestly remarked. "And the lyric is a masterpiece of writing."

Other Shows and Spectacles

Need it be said that the tradition of Christmas shows and spectacles in New York is an old one? In 1830 a New York City wax museum advertised a Christmas Eve enactment of "the Crucifixion of our Saviour on Mount Calvary, comprising about thirty figures," and another Museum offered "the Deities of Java." Since then Christmas has been the occasion for special shows, ice extravaganzas, bloody action movies, etc. However, certain traditional spectacles have, year after year, resonated with a special New York ambiance.

THE CHILDREN'S MAGICAL DEPARTURE IN
GEORGE BALANCHINE'S *THE NUTCRACKER.*

THE CHRISTMAS SHOW AT RADIO CITY

To begin with, there has always been (or at least it *seems* like "always") the Radio City Music Hall Christmas Show. The Christmas show began in 1933 with the Rockettes doing their now hoary "Parade of the Toy Soldiers" routine. The show was the inspiration of a Romanian ballet dancer named Leonid Leonidoff. In 1939, Leonidoff, who became the producer of the Radio City stage shows, added a "Living Nativity" tableau with animals. Both the toy soldiers and the Nativity have been an integral part of the live Christmas program ever since.

The Christmas show is a tremendous challenge to produce, what with dozens of cast members, lots of cos-

ROCKETTES TUMBLE IN THE TRADITIONAL
TOY SOLDIER NUMBER.

tumes and all the scenery—plus the goats and camels needed for the Nativity. With a show that has required the coordination of several dozen stagehands, various beasts, and innumerable humans, "it's just one crisis after another," the harried stage director told a *Times* reporter one year, "until, thank God, Jesus is born." In addition to committing indiscretions on stage, the camels have been known to get bored and simply walk off during everyone else's rapt contemplation of the Christ Child. They also don't like kneeling to pay homage to the infant Jesus. For a while, therefore, phony kneeling camels ("roll-ons") were trundled on stage to take the place of live ones. On the other hand, the donkeys, being donkeys, sometimes won't leave even *after* the scene is over. A good Christmas season engagement, a Radio City management spokeswoman suggested some years ago, was when there were no animal problems "other than slobbering on the Rockettes and an occasional stampede in the wings."

The Rockettes' toy soldier routine always climaxes by their falling over *backwards* in a long row. This is not a particularly easy or altogether riskless maneuver, and to make things easier, it became customary for a beefy stagehand just off-stage to catch the last Rockette to fall backwards. (The original costumes for the routine were designed back in 1933 by Vincente Minelli, father of you-know-who.)

For many years the Music Hall showed movies, and so the stage show was combined with a film. This was a familiar combination at most big movie palaces in the days before chopped-up multiplexes. As their Christmas movie in 1937, the Radio City owners, in an act of faith in Walt Disney, booked his first full-length animated feature film without even seeing it. It was *Snow White and the Seven Dwarfs*, and it was of course a smash hit, setting Disney firmly on his full-length feature career. (Though baby expert Dr. Benjamin Spock later recounted *a propos* of the film's scary parts that "Nelson Rockefeller [who started *his* career as rental agent for his father's Rockefeller Center] told my wife a long time ago that they had to reupholster the seats in Radio City Music Hall because they were wet so often by frightened children.")

But the gigantic (5,874 seats) Radio City Music Hall, with its staff of 600, plus dormitory (for the Rockettes), cafeteria, library, etc. was always expensive to run. Everything is on a huge scale. For example, the three big stage elevators on which the gigantic scenery and figures go up and down were studied by the Navy in the Thirties, which then built the technology into its aircraft carriers. (The Navy supposedly stationed a military man in the Hall during World War II to prevent enemy agents from discovering the secret of the lifts' construction.) So when the Music Hall's annual five million visitors dropped to two million by the mid-1970s due to changing tastes in film and live entertainment, the hall ran at a loss.

The Christmas stage show, however, was never junked. Instead, it was revamped in 1978 and then jazzed up again in 1985 by a man who produced Super Bowl half-time shows. It made too much money to be jettisoned. Industry insiders estimate that the show grossed $40 million in 1995, while the whole rest of the year's shows at Radio City brought in only $20 million. Ya gotta love it—well, maybe not if you're Holden Caulfield. In *The Catcher in the Rye* he sarcastically dismissed "all these angels... coming out of the boxes and everywhere, guys carrying crucifixes and stuff all over the place" in "this Christmas thing they have at Radio City every year." "Yeah," said Holden, "big deal."

A CHRISTMAS CAROL

Since 1994 there has been competition for Radio City's Christmas show in the form of the annual Madison Square Garden musical production of Dickens' *A Christmas Carol*. The *Carol* has employed the talents of Broadway and movie set designer Tony Walton (*A Funny Thing Happened on the Way to the Forum, Guys and Dolls*), song writer Alan Menken (Disney's *The Little Mermaid* and *Beauty and the Beast*, choreographer Susan Stroman (*Crazy for You*), and, recently, Tony Randall (as the old skinflint Ebenezer S.) to put together a production for the gigantic (5,600 seats) theater at Madison Square Garden. The idea seems to be maximum activity—almost 500 costumes, ninety players, etc. The Ghost of Christmas Past has been given white powdered, top-hatted *assistants*, with strobe lights in their navels (don't ask), plus there are, uh, tap-dancing ladies dressed as fruits who strip down to tarty versions of the Rockettes to join with the Ghost of Christmas Present to show Scrooge that Christmas is *fun*. As your program will inform you, the spirits who pop up at one point from

SCROOGE AND FRIENDS IN MADISON SQUARE GARDEN'S
A CHRISTMAS CAROL.

forty presumably infernal trap doors have to contend with a crawl space only four feet high under the stage because the Madison Square Garden theater is built over New York City's Amtrak station. In fact, set designer Walton described the theater as having "the quality of around seventeen Ramada Inns squashed together." Oh, and artificial snow drops on the audience at the production's end as, with Scrooge's resolve not to let his life be ruled by money ringing in their ears, theatergoers are reminded over the p.a. system to patronize the souvenir shops on the way out.

Indeed, the marketing of *A Christmas Carol* is to ordinary marketing as World War II is to a boxing match. Last year American Express, which sponsors the show, sent out mailings publicizing it to 500,000 card holders, 10,000,000 Pathmark shopping bags carried the show's logo (trademarked, naturally), and millions of McDonald's trays bore paper liners emblazoned with the logo. As at Radio City Music Hall, other seasonal shows, including *The Wizard of Oz*, are materializing at the Garden, and there are plans to have road companies. "We do not view *A Christmas Carol* as competition," said a Radio City marketing person darkly after the Music Hall—surely by coincidence?—cut its seven-minute "Christmas Carol" segment.

GEORGE BALANCHINE'S THE NUTCRACKER

In the St. Petersburg of the early 1900s, the young George Balanchivadze entered the famous imperial academy for the Tsar's young ballet students in training. Taking classes as well in regular school subjects, the boys at the Theater Street School all wore uniforms like those of military cadets. They were, after all, considered as much in the Tsar's service as students in military training, except that they wore on their collars a lyre, the instrument sacred to Apollo, god of music. *The Nutcracker* formed part of a trio of ballets (along with *Swan Lake* and *Sleeping Beauty*), written by Tchaikovsky for the master choreographer of the Maryinsky Theatre, Marius Petipa, and his collaborator Lev Ivanov. Balanchivadze (he would later change his name to "Balanchine") grew up loving Tchaikovsky, and in *The Nutcracker* he danced the Mouse King and the Nutcracker Prince.

Balanchine left Russia and ultimately came to the United States under the aegis of Lincoln Kirstein. After various undertakings, including choreographing Broadway musicals, he became the director of the New York City Ballet. On the stage of City Center at 55th Street the company put on short pieces that Balanchine choreographed to the music of Schoenberg and Stravinsky in an "abstract" dance style that drew the raves of the discerning—but sold (relatively) few tickets.

The director of City Center was former alderman Morton Baum, an amateur musician who, as Mayor LaGuardia's tax counsel in the mid-1930s, had devised New York City's first sales tax. Baum was worried that Balanchine's ballets, wonderful as they were, did not bring in enough money. However, the 1940 Walt Dis-

*M*ORTON BAUM—
WHO PUSHED FOR
THE NUTCRACKER.

ney film *Fantasia* had featured an animated "Nutcracker Suite" (the arrangement Tchaikovsky had culled from the ballet) with dancing Asian mushrooms, whirling flowers, and other animated exotica. (Balanchine had actually watched *Fantasia* in the company of a horrified Igor Stravinsky, whose *Sacre du Printemps* Disney had turned into a promenade for dinosaurs.) And in 1944 the Ballets Russes put on a production of *The Nutcracker* in America, albeit with adults cast as the children who appear in the first act, and the same year there was a full-length version in San Francisco on which Balanchine advised.

Okay. "Morton Baum always said to me, 'George, do *Nutcracker*,'" Balanchine recalled, "and finally I say, 'OK, but not the lousy way Ballets Russes do it with no children.' So I begin to think about how to make it like it was in Russia when I was a child…. *The Nutcracker* is a ballet about Christmas. We used to have a fantastic Christmas in Petersburg," Balanchine recalled. "St. Petersburg was all dark and somehow strange" and in the big Christmas services at the great cathedrals there was "an unforgettable moment of mystery: when the candles were put out, the church was plunged into darkness, and the choir came in."

Balanchine went to work re-creating the old Petipa production he had danced in as a boy. He changed and modernized it, sometimes altering the name of a character, adding the reindeer to take the children away at the end of the last act, and, of course, as he vowed, putting in real children instead of adult dancers disguised as kids in the first act. The production premiered in February 1954, became an instant classic (all eight scheduled performances actually sold out in advance), and had to be repeated in November. *Herald Tribune* critic Edwin Denby called the production a "smash hit…a family spectacle, large and leisurely, that lasts two hours and sends people home refreshed and happy." It has been a Christmas favorite— and money-maker for the New York City Ballet—ever since. Indeed, Balanchine once considered sending out *Nutcracker* troupes on tour six months a year.

Not that there weren't problems. *Children?* "When Balanchine decided to use children we all thought, 'Oh, God save us,'" remembered an early New York City Ballet member. "They were everywhere underfoot, like newborn kittens. The halls were swarming with children." The City Center was a difficult theater for ballet troupes anyway since it had, as Balanchine's patron Lincoln Kirstein remarked, "literally no offstage room." And Balanchine also insisted on a *tree*, a real three-dimensional tree, and, in fact, spent much of the show's budget just on the tree. "And Baum says, 'George, you fool, that's too much money,' and I say, 'We're not awful like Ballets Russes. The tree is the ballerina.'" But on the small stage of City Center with no trap door, what to do? A collapsible tree that could be hauled up by a rope was the answer.

Problems, problems. The tree's lights short-circuited, fizzed, and smoked, and the tree itself sometimes got stuck and obstinately refused to rise. The delicate snowfall that closed Act I with the ethereal Waltz of the Snowflakes also created difficulties, since the phony snow was swept up and reused after each performance. Since everything *else* was swept up with the snow, too, the dancers consequently found contact lenses, nails, and other detritus sometimes swirling down on them along with artificial snowflakes.

About 100,000 people see Balanchine's *The Nutcracker* at the New York City Ballet each year (except when prevented by strikes, as in 1973 and 1976). In 1994 it was even made into a film. Inspired by the ballet's success, ballet companies throughout America have followed New York City Ballet's example if not always Balanchine's choreography. Meanwhile, even in a world of high-tech special effects, fascinated audiences still marvel at the ingenious Balanchine touches of stagecraft that survive the master. For example, in the second act he introduced a tricky gimmick for the Sugar Plum Fairy, who perches on point and then seems to glide magically across the floor without moving. How? Because she is actually standing on a movable piece of tin that is drawn across the stage floor by a wire offstage, a device which Balanchine remembered from his pre-Revolutionary days in Russia. And the magical bed that slides across the floor with little Marie in it when she dreams? Ah—but it is wrong to spoil all the magic.

THE MESSIAH

But enough of spectacle—

For straight-out resounding musical oom-pah at Christmas-time, it seems nothing can beat the *Messiah*, which is strange, because, it was, after all, written for Easter.

The association of the *Messiah* with New York City goes back years and years. The first American performance of the *Messiah* (or rather a part thereof, namely, "an Extract from the late Mr. Handel's Grand Oratorio, called the Messiah, consisting of the Overture, and sixteen other Pieces, viz. Airs, Recitatives and Choruses") took place in the Music Room of the New York City Tavern on Broadway, tickets eight shillings, on January 16, 1770, which was two years before it was first heard in Europe. In 1841, diarist George Strong went to St. Peter's Church in the city ("Church jammed," he noted in his diary) for Christmas services and heard "a choir of 50 or so—well drilled …choir & the full organ…the Hallelujah Chorus at the end

THE MESSIAH SING-IN AT AVERY FISHER HALL.

of the services was great…" Mammoth choral singing was something of a fad in the mid-1800s. In 1873 Leopold Damrosch founded the New York Oratorio Society, which performed the *Messiah* every Christmas, with Andrew Carnegie becoming a staunch partisan of the organization. In fact, the Society's performances were held in Carnegie's living room until he decided to build the group its own hall in 1891. Since then, the *Messiah* has been performed faithfully each year at, yes, Carnegie Hall by the Oratorio Society in a continuing tradition.

The emphasis until relatively recently was always on the need for training before performing Handel's piece, given what sophisticated music it was. Then in 1967 one Martin Josman inaugurated a "Messiah Sing-In," picking up on the "teach-in" and "sit-in" language of the Sixties. His innovation spread to other cities. ("Messiah Sing-In" is now a registered trademark, no less). It is this "Sing-In" which now engulfs Lincoln Center's Avery Fisher Hall each holiday as several thousand people swarm into the building to bull their way through the old German's heavenly choral music. Everybody is segregated according to type of voice and the numerous conductors conduct away, hoping for the best and trying to leaven the sluggish tempo that inevitably attends any large-scale choral singing by unrehearsed groups.

TUBA CONCERT

And speaking of music...

What about the concert of dozens of tubas held every year during the holiday season in Rockefeller Plaza? The event had its origins in 1974 when Harvey Philips, a tuba instructor at Indiana University, decided to honor a tuba teacher who had been born Christmas Day, 1902. A fitting honor, possibly, to be devised by a tuba enthusiast like Philips, who, in addition to playing with the New York Philharmonic, the Metropolitan Opera, and the New York City Ballet orchestra, had left college to join the Ringling Brothers and Barnum & Bailey Circus Band.

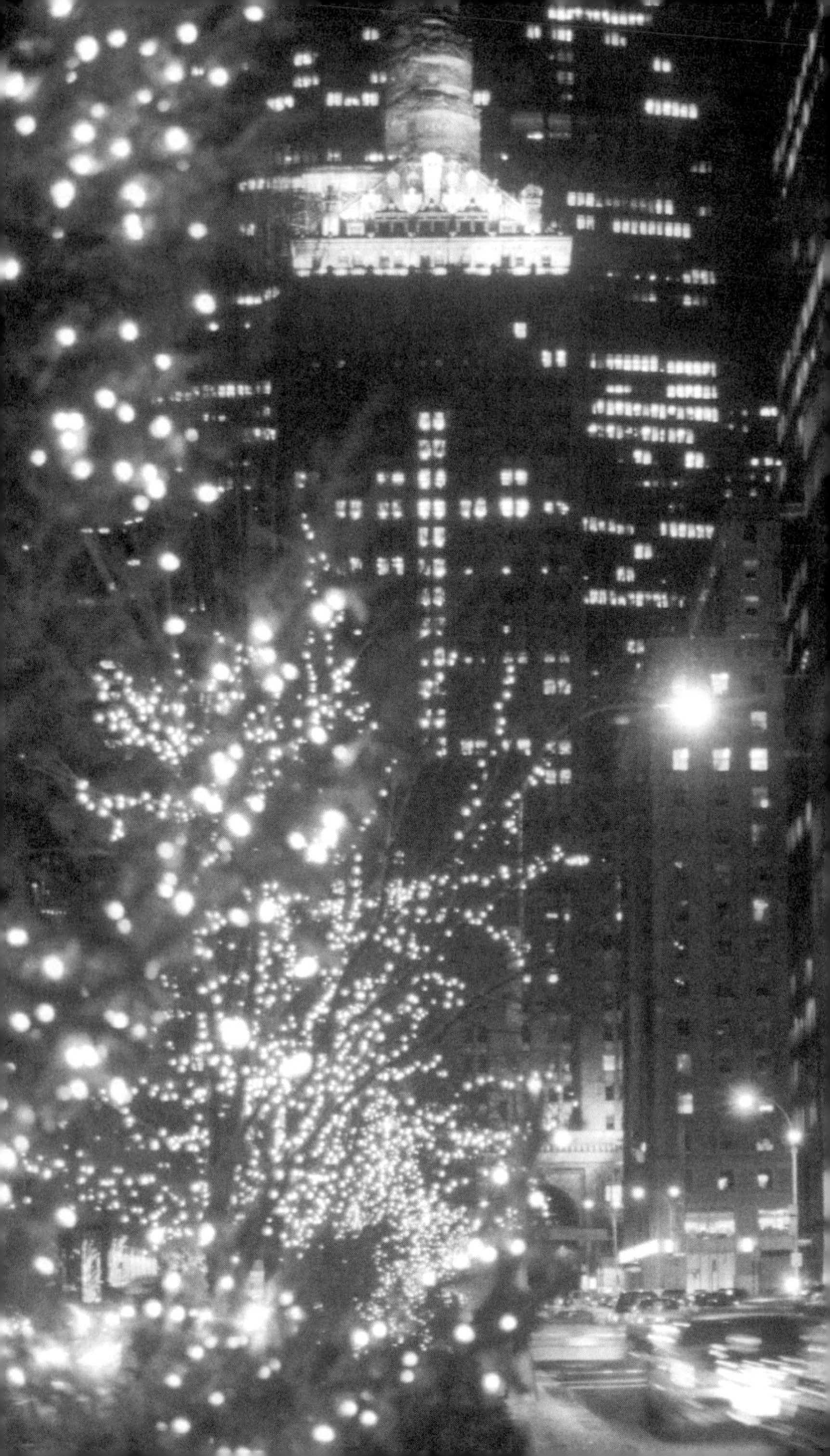

$\mathcal{P}$ARK $\mathcal{A}$VENUE

After so much noise and spectacle, what better than some respite somewhere, away from the holiday rush and madness. Park Avenue, perhaps? It glitters at Christmastime with a host of white lights, big and small, which have somehow a refreshing chastity after the extravagance and glitz of Fifth Avenue, perhaps, too, a suggestion of the self-important gravity appropriate to all enclaves of great wealth, and surely, as well, a touch of melancholy.

Park Avenue's holiday garb is not, of course, the work of Santa and his elves. Mrs. Stephen C. Clark

103

(whose family was heir to the Singer Sewing machine fortune and built the famous Dakota apartment house on Manhattan's West Side) lost a son in World War II. So, in December 1945, aided by several friends who had also lost children in the war, she had thirty lighted Christmas trees put on the avenue's median strips as a memorial to those New Yorkers who had died in World War II. (Corporate and individual donors have now taken over the financing of the trees.) Originally the trees stretched from 96th Street down to 34th Street, each bearing lights colored white and yellow, instead of the normal Christmassy red and green, so the tree lights could not be mistaken for traffic lights. (Starting in 1982, the cherry and hawthorn trees that grow on the medians year-round have also been lit, to celebrate Hanukkah.) Each year now on the first Sunday in December the Christmas trees are lit in a ceremony at the Brick Church on 91st Street and Park Avenue that mixes the playing of "Taps" and Christmas carols. The lights come on in sequence south down the avenue to 48th Street and north up to 96th in a moment that many Park Avenue dwellers commemorate with parties and shouted greetings of "Merry Christmas!" out their windows.

A few years after the Christmas trees were first erected, the New York Central railroad company created in the windows of their thirty-story headquarters building at the southern end of the main vista of Park Avenue a giant shining white cross 138 feet high and forty-eight feet wide. Although it appeared to be the product of interior office illumination, it was actually created with thirty-two spe-

*P*ARK AVENUE AT CHRISTMASTIME.

cial 300-watt lamps. The big lights were placed, one per window, across eight windows on the 25th floor and then, two windows wide, down from the 28th to the 17th floors. When the building was later acquired by the late Harry Helmsley of the Helmsley hotels fame, he renamed it by changing two letters in "N.Y. Central" to make the structure the "N.Y. General" building. ("General" signified nothing—substituting "G" for "C" and "e" for "t" was just the cheapest way to alter the lettering on the building's facade.) His company maintained the lit cross tradition in the windows of what was subsequently renamed "The Helmsley Building."

The New York Central ran the Grand Central Terminal station at 42nd Street and owned much of the land on which the apartments along Park Avenue stood because it controlled the railroad tracks and tunnels underneath leading to the terminal. However, railroads gave way to trucks and planes in post-World-War-II America. So the railroad company replaced many of the relatively low-rent apartment buildings on Park Avenue between 42nd and 59th Streets with high-rent-yielding office buildings to make up for the revenue loss it was suffering from the other modes of transportation. Unlike older skyscrapers like the Empire State and Chrysler Buildings, the new structures were in the "boxy" plain Modernist style that seemed to almost require decoration. They were also often owned by companies that made consumer products—Lever House (soap), the Seagram building (whiskey), and the Pepsi Cola building (soft drinks)—and so presumably cared about presenting a pleasant face to the man in the street in a way that the Empire State and other older skyscrapers did not.

The Pepsi Cola building at 500 Park Avenue on the southwest corner of 59th Street (long since relinquished as the company's headquarters and renamed) was decorated with a seventy-foot long string of 25,000 red, blue, silver, and green Christmas tree balls meant to represent Christmas ribbon candy. And in 1958 Gene Moore, of the Tiffany windows, was commissioned to do a Christmas arrangement for the Seagram building on 53rd Street and set up 350 little trees in the two fountains outside the building. He then decorated them with 12,000 miniature white lights in keeping with the Park Avenue Christmas lighting color scheme already set by the New York Central cross and the Christmas tree lights on the median strips. (The tiny white lights, which were reflected in the shallow waters of the Seagram building's pools, apparently initiated the widespread fashion for the use of tiny white bulbs at Christmas as somehow more "chic" than full-size colored tree bulbs.)

At Christmastime in 1953 a revolving carousel, rented from an amusement park, was erected in the showroom at the base of the Lever House mini-skyscraper at 54th Street (with, originally, different Lever products, e.g. Lux soap, whirling around on the carousel instead of riders; they were ultimately replaced with presents). In 1969, Lever Brothers stopped renting and commissioned its own carousel. This pleasant structure, with its eight standing and six galloping horses, is installed and assembled each year on the night before Thanksgiving and decorated during the following week.

"WHITE CHRISTMAS"—From the white lights of Park Avenue to the "White Christmas" of Irving Berlin. A stroll several blocks east of Park Avenue brings one to Beekman Place, a wealthy enclave of small, sedate townhouses and dig-

THE LEVER HOUSE CAROUSEL, 1961.

nified apartment buildings overlooking the East River. Since 1967, a composer and singer named John Wallowitch has gathered with friends each Christmas to sing "White Christmas" and "Always" outside the small townhouse at No. 17

Beekman Place that from 1946 until his death in 1989 was the home of the reclusive popular song composer Irving Berlin. (In 1983 when Wallowitch plucked up the courage to ring the Berlins' doorbell, the Yuletide singers were invited in, and Berlin himself, in bathrobe and slippers, spoke with them in his kitchen, telling them it was "the nicest Christmas present I've ever had.")

*I*RVING BERLIN

It is perhaps typical of New York—and of America—that a cantor's son who emigrated to the United States from Russia in 1893 as a young boy wrote one of the country's most popular Christmas songs. One evening in early 1941, Berlin, already the world famous author of "Alexander's Ragtime Band," "Easter Parade," and countless other songs, was working away on holiday material for a new film. The memory of spending Christmas in Los Angeles and of missing snow came back to him forcefully, and he began writing, wrote, in fact, until the sun came up. He told his transcriber as he hurried into his office early the next morning that it was "the best song *anybody* ever wrote." It was, Berlin recalled later, one of the rare songs that he didn't have to work for, sweat over, or force, but that seemed to well up, all of a piece. He called it "White Christmas."

At a time when intermarriage of Jews and Gentiles was socially impermissible, Berlin had married Ellin Mackay, the daughter of a wealthy Catholic telegraph magnate whose 648-acre Long Island estate boasted 50 rooms and a staff of 134. Mr. Mackay and Ellin's friends opposed her union with Berlin. But the marriage was a happy one— and each December Mrs. Berlin would read the children the story of Judas Maccabeus and light the candles for Hanukkah. Then a few days later she would read them the Gospel according to St. Luke. On Christmas Day Berlin himself would tell his children the story of how as a small boy on the Lower East Side he would furtively cross the street to gaze in wonder at the Christmas tree of the neighboring O'Hara family.

"White Christmas" was featured in the 1942 film *Holiday Inn*. Bing Crosby sang it as he tried to start a rustic getaway open only on holidays. Journalists and Berlin's employees were skeptical about the song's quality and prospects, and the songwriter was depressed. Then American servicemen around the world began deluging G.I. radio stations with requests for the Christmas song that reminded them of home and a gentler, more peaceful time. The song won Berlin a 1942 Academy Award and by 1951 had sold fourteen million records (it became the composer's most popular song). And, yes, the movie *Holiday Inn* was such a great favorite of one Kemmons Wilson, who pioneered the first, family-oriented chain of motels in the mid-1950s, that he decided to name his hostelries after the film.

Is there a touch of wistfulness, almost of melancholy, about "White Christmas"? Christmas was always celebrated with great fanfare in the Berlin household, yet Irving Berlin and his wife mysteriously left the house each Christmas Eve. It was not until she was ten years old that one of the Berlins' daughters accidentally stumbled upon a hidden newspaper clipping that revealed why: it was to visit the grave of their son, Irving Berlin, Jr.—who had died on Christmas Day, 1928, three weeks after his birth. Christmas? Years later, when the little girl had grown up, Mrs. Berlin remarked offhandedly to her daughter one day, "Oh, you know, I hated Christmas, we both hated Christmas. We only did it for you children."

The
Museums

THE METROPOLITAN'S CHRISTMAS TREE—
There is a quiet beauty about some of the city's
holiday traditions that can be surprising in the midst of
such a bustling, noisy city. And some of the more impressive are perhaps the big elaborately decorated trees at
New York's museums. Here chronology—and perhaps
over-all impact—would seem to concede pride of place
to the one at the Metropolitan Museum of Art.

Loretta Hines was the daughter of a lumber baron
from Chicago. When she married paper manufacturer

113

LORETTA HINES HOWARD, DONOR OF AND
MOVING SPIRIT BEHIND THE METROPOLITAN
MUSEUM OF ART'S NATIVITY CHRISTMAS TREE.

Howell Howard in 1924 her mother gave her a creche with three figures from Marshall Field's in Chicago. When her husband died in 1937 Mrs. Howard moved to New York and studied with the Ashcan School painter Robert Henri. Her work was in several gallery shows. As time went on, Howard also added to her collection of creche figures, which she arranged every year around the family Christmas tree.

The creche tradition goes back centuries. A nativity scene appeared on early sarcophagi, and St. Francis is credited with having devised a life-size creche with a live ox and actors for the villagers of Greccio in 1223. But the chief center of the cult of the creche, or *presepio*, as it was called, was Naples. In the latter half of the 18th century, well-to-do families hired artists who went to elaborate lengths each Christmas to construct hosts of figures. Whole floors in private homes were given over to the creche displays, and families went from house to house during the Christmas season to see them. To add to the collections, artists were hired who could create animals, humans or angels as occasion and taste demanded. The King of Naples in 1734 alone was said to have had almost six thousand figures.

Many of the collections were scattered after Naples was united with Italy in 1861. However, Mrs. Howard was told by then Metropolitan Museum director Francis Taylor of

DETAIL OF CRECHE AT THE METROPOLITAN MUSEUM'S "ANGEL TREE."

Eugenio Catello, who had one of the best collections of creche figures in the world. She corresponded with Catello for some time, eventually arranging for the purchase of the figures she wanted. In 1957 and 1958 she assembled the tree with figures at the Met, whereupon the museum was deluged with calls asking when her collection would be displayed again. Coincidentally, she was finding caring for the figures in the basement of her house on East 74th Street increasingly onerous. So in 1964 she donated some 140 figures, including many from the Catello collection, to the Met, whose conservation department, she was confident, could adequately maintain them. She added a few more each year, and she took charge of arranging the Met's tree.

As Mrs. Howard pointed out, "The Christmas tree is a Northern European tradition, and the creche is a Southern European tradition." The display, appropriately, given New York's tradition of ethnic diversity, blends the German tree and the Italian creche. The creche figures' heads are terra cotta but their limbs are wood, and wire and hemp inside the bodies make them partially flexible. The figures are arranged and suspended from the top of the thirty-foot tree down. Then the branches are added and finally the lights. For years Mrs. Howard, who died in 1982, was assisted in arranging the tree by her daughter. Now, assisted in turn by *her* daughter, Ms. Linn Howard each year directs the setting up of the tree, frequently adding new figures she has acquired so that from year to year the arrangement is never the same. Erecting and trimming the tree usually takes about three weeks, during which time the Medieval Sculpture Hall, where the tree is set up, is blocked off.

THE MUSEUM OF NATURAL HISTORY—In 1973, the American Museum of Natural History offered its own gigantic Christmas tree, but it was decorated with origami, that is, paper folded according to an old Asian tradition in the shape of objects and animals. The museums's first origami tree, with only some thirty models on it, was the work of Alice Gray, a scientific assistant in the entomology department of the Museum. Among other things, Ms. Gray handled calls about bugs and the like to the Museum from the public. "Yesterday a neurosurgeon called from California," she cheerily told an interviewer one December. "He was worried because his tarantula hadn't eaten since April."

Because it had an insect on the cover, she picked up a book on origami one day. Intrigued, she began making origami figures and eventually created a four-foot high tree for her office at Christmas one year with insects made from envelope linings. A trustee learned of the tree and asked her to do a larger one for the whole museum, and so the origami tree was born. Today, the fourteen-foot (it was originally twenty-five feet) tall tree generally holds somewhere in the neighborhood of 1,000 pieces of origami.

The Museum boasts an even more venerable Christmas tradition. In 1900, Frank Chapman, the Museum's former curator of ornithology, initiated a Christmas bird count, which is now conducted each Yuletide by bird-watchers all over the country. His goal was to replace *shooting* birds, then a popular holiday practice, with *looking* at them. Central Park was the site of one of the counts that first year ("American Herring Gull, 12; Downy Woodpecker, 1; Starling, 4 [singing]; White-throated Sparrow, abundant [twice heard singing]; Song Sparrow, 2; Robin, 1").

ALICE GRAY, BUG DOYENNE AND ORIGINATOR OF THE ORIGAMI TREE.

Museum goers throughout the world can thank Chapman for also inventing the habitat display, in which stuffed creatures are arranged in a lifelike exhibit in a verisimilitudinous habitat. Prior to Chapman, stuffed museum specimens were simply listlessly displayed in glass cases.

THE ORIGAMI TREE AT THE AMERICAN
MUSEUM OF NATURAL HISTORY.

$\mathcal{W}$hat of Christmas at the other museums? The Museum of Modern Art, with that sometimes rather grim penchant for education that distinguished its founding director, Alfred Barr, ran a Christmas Holiday Carnival of Modern Art for some years beginning in 1942. For a modest admissions charge plus a "materials fee," a boy or girl (some 2,400 in 1949) entered a child-sized gate leading to two galleries on the second floor of the museum. One gallery offered toys, sculpture, and the like that children could touch. (For the 1945 carnival Alexander Calder made a cow that wiggled its tail.) And in the second room there were art supplies and work spaces where children could make a "creative" mess using paints, pipe cleaners, paste, colored paper, and iron and magnets.

By a strange irony, one of the great testaments to the transcendent importance of love and charity over the pursuit of money reposes in the former New York City personal library building of the man whose name, perhaps more than any other, was synonymous for decades in the United States with wealth and financial power. Sometime between 1890 and 1900, J.P. Morgan bought the original manuscript of *A Christmas Carol* from a Dickens collector who had paid £300 for it. The collector had himself acquired it in a chain that stretched back to a friend of

Dickens to whom the writer had originally given it after having it bound in red leather. Now each year at Christmastime the manuscript—"My own, and only, MS of the book," as Dickens thoughtfully wrote on the title page—in the same binding that the author had made for it, is placed on exhibit by the Pierpont Morgan Library at the imposing edifice on East 36th Street.

The New York Historical Society boasts a copy of "'Twas the Night Before Christmas" in author Clement Moore's own handwriting that was written out in March 1862 at the request of the Society's librarian. The Society exhibits the manuscript from time to time at Christmas (not each year, because of its fragility). However, every year during the holidays it displays the desk at which Moore is said to have written the poem.

TELEVISON AND THE NEW YORK CHRISTMAS

A nd so to bed—or television.

Television has played a powerful role in bringing the New York Christmas to both New Yorkers and out-of-towners alike, perhaps, indeed, helping to make the city a holiday destination for more and more people from all over the country. Guy Lombardo's New Year's dance music was first televised in 1943, the Macy's parade in 1948, and the Rockefeller Center tree lighting in 1951 on *The Kate Smith Show*, when the ample songstress herself pushed the button to light the ever-

DECEMBER 1946. *IT'S A WONDERFUL LIFE*
WORLD PREMIERE AT THE NOW DEFUNCT GLOBE
THEATER, 47TH STREET AND BROADWAY.

green. (In 1954, four kids on a telecast of *The Howdy Doody Show* pushed the button.)

Of course in those early days New York was the center of the TV universe. Not only were ABC, CBS, and NBC based in the city in the late Forties, but two-thirds of the sets in existence in the United States belonged to viewers in the New York metropolitan area, which is one reason why so much of the early programming, e.g., the shows of comics like Sid Caesar, Milton Berle, or Jackie Gleason, had a strong New York ethnic flavor.

In those long ago days, however, the major commercial networks actually competed to bring classical music, as well as their regular, schlocky programming, to the American public. So it was that in 1951, Samuel Chotznikoff, a former music critic for the *New York Post* who was married to Jascha Heifetz's sister, for $5,000 commissioned a Christmas opera from Gian Carlo Menotti on behalf of NBC. Menotti was a young composer, prodigiously talented, working in many media, including radio, and his music was *accessible*. Or, as an excited fan said, rushing up to compliment him after one of the Broadway performances of his opera *The Consul*, "I was afraid that this was going to be an opera."

Menotti was slow to come up with an idea for the holiday work NBC had commissioned. As the days wound down, he found nothing coming to mind until, so he said later, he wandered through the Metropolitan Museum of Art one November afternoon and happened to pass Hieronymus Bosch's "The Adoration of the Magi."

It started the wheels turning.

A boy, lame; his mother; and mysterious visitors—on their way, it turns out, to do homage to the new-born Christ child. Menotti had a title, too, although at first no one liked it. He called Chotznikoff after dinner on Thanksgiving and said "I'm going to call the opera *Amahl and the Night Visitors*." That night Menotti began to write. As a small boy in Italy, he and his brother had stayed up late waiting for the Three Kings (the Italian equivalent of Santa Claus) to bring them gifts, hearing the silver bridles jingling on the kings' camels as they passed through the streets at night. The kings became central figures in the opera, as did the lame boy healed by a miracle. The lad had special meaning for the composer. As a boy, Menotti himself had once been crippled. But then his nurse took him to the shrine of a Madonna credited with miraculous power where Menotti received a blessing before the image. He was cured within a short time.

Amahl, broadcast on Christmas Eve, miraculously without any interrupting commercials, was an immense hit, seen by an estimated thirteen million viewers. Callers jammed the phone lines to NBC within minutes after the broadcast demanding copies of the score. The opera was repeated reg-

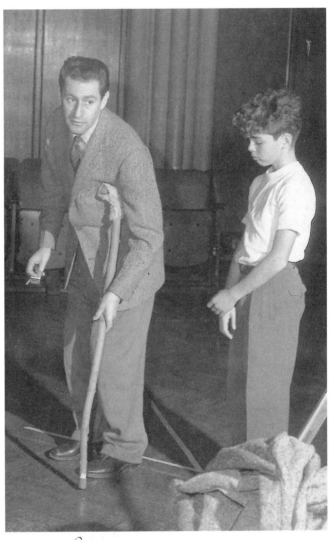

COMPOSER GIAN CARLO MENOTTI
REHEARSING THE FIRST AMAHL FOR THE PREMIERE
OF *AMAHL AND THE NIGHT VISITORS*, IN 1951.

ularly at Christmastime thereafter. When it was presented on Christmas Eve, 1953, this time in color, it became the first commercially broadcast color production in the United States, though, given the small number of color sets then, most viewers saw it only in black and white.

Menotti had no illusions about Amahl: he tells lies, he is mischievous, and he is no angel, Menotti used to say. Perhaps that is one reason he remained so popular. On the opera's thirtieth anniversary Menotti reported that the work brought him countless letters from children. "Dear Mr. Menotti: Last night I saw *Amahl and the Night Visitors* and it is the first opera I've ever seen and I think it is the best" or, when Menotti had announced plans to quit the theater, "Please go on fighting. I have a good story for an opera which I can give you for nothing. It's about Amahl going to New York after Bethlehem and getting sick again. But it's not as gloomy as it sounds."

THE NUTCRACKER—In 1958, CBS broadcast an hour-long version of Balanchine's *The Nutcracker* (with Balanchine playing Drosselmeyer). This helped enormously to spread the Balanchine interpretation across the United States, in part by allowing choreographers elsewhere in the country to observe what Balanchine had done with the piece. Mikhail Baryshnikov, who for a time danced with Balanchine's New York City Ballet, choreographed his own version of *The Nutcracker* for the American Ballet Theatre. It has been shown regularly on TV at Christmas.

IT'S A WONDERFUL LIFE—This holiday favorite about the small-town businessman who is about to take his life until a guardian angel shows him the positive impact he has had on his community has, surprisingly, a New York City origin. For the movie began as a short story by the balding, bespectacled Philip Van Doren Stern, anthologist, sometime novelist, and former advertising man, who spent most of his life in Manhattan, Brooklyn, and New Jersey. Stern worked as an editor for Pocket Books, designed books for Alfred Knopf, and headed the book manufacturing department of Simon & Schuster. Shaving one morning in February 1938, he suddenly had an idea for a story about a man tempted to commit suicide who is saved by an angel who shows him how different the lives of his fellow townspeople would have been without him. Excited, Stern wrote it down, then abandoned it, but then over several years tried reworking it. His agent sent it to various magazines, all of which turned it down. Finally, one Christmas Stern had a version of the story printed up as an extended Christmas card and sent it to 200 friends. One of them was a Hollywood agent, who sold it to RKO Pictures, at the instigation, it is said, of Cary Grant, who purportedly wanted to play the lead. But then the story was re-sold to director Frank Capra, newly returned from World War II and looking for projects for his new production company, and Capra cast James Stewart in the lead.

In that era movies opened first in New York. So the film had its world premiere at the now-vanished Globe Theater on 47th Street and Broadway in Times Square (right next door to the city's very first Automat) on December 20, 1946. Despite good reviews, however, reaction to the film was not impressive, and its financial fortunes were unremarkable. In fact, far from becoming a holiday favorite, it did so badly that in 1974, when its copyright expired, no one even bothered to renew it—which turned out to be a magic turning point. Television stations all around the country began showing it at Christmas after they realized they did not have to pay for it. Helped immeasurably by this wide exposure, the film soon became a holiday classic.

MIRACLE ON 34TH STREET—And what of that equally stalwart holiday fare, *Miracle on 34th Street*, the 1947 film (re-made in 1994) that told the tale of the Macy's department store executives and the little girl who didn't believe in Santa even when they found him—or his doppelganger—in their midst? The idea for *Miracle* apparently came from a weekend collaboration. One participant was screenwriter Valentine Davies, the son of a prominent New York real estate magnate (whose last name a young actress and favorite of William Randolph Hearst named

A YOUNG NATALIE WOOD AND FRIEND CONTEMPLATE CHRISTMAS WITH THE MACY'S PARADE IN THE BACKGROUND IN THE 1947 *MIRACLE ON 34TH STREET*.

Marion Douras took for her own to become "Marion Davies," who was memorably caricatured in *Citizen Kane* as a talentless opera singer.) The other was screenwriter-director George Seaton, who had written screenplays for the Marx Brothers.

What about Santa Claus comes to town and finds out how commercial everything is, Davies suggested? Better, said Seaton—how about a guy who comes back to town who *thinks* he's Santa? For eighteen months they worked away at the story. *Miracle* was then filmed in four weeks at the Fox studios in Los Angeles and New York. Actor Edmund Gwenn, who was playing "Kris Kringle," actually sat enthroned as Santa on a float in the real 1946 Macy's Thanksgiving Day Parade, with Fox cameramen concealed along the route to catch the action for editing into the film.

However, Daryl Zanuck, the head of Twentieth Century Fox, was not enthusiastic about the film and accordingly had the movie released in *June* of 1947. Despite the studio's efforts to torpedo the film, it was a hit. The *Times* reviewer, Bosley Crowther, called it "the freshest little picture in a long time, and maybe even the best comedy of this year." (And "most amusing," he said, is "little Natalie Wood as the child who has been trained to sniff at Santa…") Fox eventually wised up and leased the film out each

Christmas to TV stations for holiday showings that brought in about $1 million over some twenty years. Customers, meanwhile, inquired whether Macy's really *did* send people to Gimbel's, as the movie suggested, if it didn't have toys that children wanted. In response, Macy's offered a comparison shopper named "Kristine Kringle." Gimbel's took out an ad congratulating Macy's on the movie, and, yielding to the power of suggestion, glitzy Texas store Neiman-Marcus sent shoppers to its arch-rival when it didn't have items customers wanted.

THE LOG—And what, alas, of *truly* memorable vanished traditions? From the semi-sublime, that is, we come to— the Yule Log. In 1966 Frederick Thrower, president of New York City's WPIX Channel 11, saw a television commercial. It inspired him to eliminate all programming on the station on Christmas Eve from 9:30 P.M. till a half-hour after midnight. And to replace it with an endless film of a burning Yule log. Why? Thrower was eloquent on the purpose of the station's selfless effort. (Channel 11 estimated their advertising loss at $4,000.) "It is our hope," he observed, "that we can restore for metropolitan New York families the kind of Christmas atmosphere that has become traditional in American life." Certainly—that old burning black-and-white log in the fireplace. For there was no color; even so, said Thrower, "the symbolic impact will be there." The log cameoed in Whit Stillman's 1990 film of WASP Christmas angst, *Metropolitan*.

The
Ghosts
of
Christmas
Past

B ut *speaking* of traditions, what of the ghosts of
Christmas Past in New York City? As late as 1964,
a reporter could still find in the traditionally German-
American community of Yorkville on the Upper East
Side at Christmas "an opulence of smoked sausages, eel,
foot-high gingerbread houses, genuine Bremen fruit
cake and show windows with old-country snow
scenes." Meanwhile, eels—seasoned, dusted with flour,
and fried—were table delicacies on Christmas Eve for
Italian-American Catholics.

1950, anyone? Barnard seniors in academic gowns
made their way, as tradition dictated, through the res-

BOY SELLING CHRISTMAS TOYS ON 14TH STREET
AROUND THE TURN OF THE CENTURY.

idence halls of the college on an evening shortly before Christmas carrying candles and singing carols. And that same year many of New York City's finest were openly letting it be known that they would appreciate Christmas gratuities from the merchants on their beat. Some of the police even thoughtfully gave the storekeepers typed lists of suggested gifts, until the police commissioner announced that there were going to be no more Christmas shakedowns.

And what about further back, say, the Roaring Twen-

*B*ARNARD COLLEGE SENIORS IN 1951
IN TRADITIONAL HOLIDAY PROCESSION
THROUGH DORMITORIES SINGING CAROLS.

ties? Big shows opening at Christmas? Well, yes—but not movies. In Christmas *week* of December 1927 no less than sixteen Broadway shows opened, eleven of them on the evening of December 26 alone. Wall Street? The Curb Exchange (now known as the American Stock Exchange) put on a show complete with a Charleston contest for its employees, while a now defunct federal agency called the Sub-Treasury located at the intersection of Nassau and Wall Streets disbursed huge amounts of newly minted money to fathers who wanted to give it to their children, fashionable jewelry stores who wanted to make bright, shiny change for their holiday customers, and similar thoughtful folk. The brokerage house of W.H. Hutton & Co. announced varying Christmas bonuses of 7-15% of one's annual salary depending on length of service, and the Standard Bank offered 2-8% bonuses. (How to spend it? Well, for one thing, in 1921 the Metropolitan Museum of Art had for the first time sent out a Christmas gift catalogue).

To handle holiday travel to New England in the pre-air shuttle days of 1926, the New York, New Haven & Hartford Railroad announced it would run 115 extra trains to get New Yorkers home to their out of town kin and would also add 253 cars to its regular trains. This, as the *New York Times* said, would be a relative cinch, "because hand baggage is used and trains and stations are not choked with trunks, as they are at the end of other holidays." To those who had come from afar and could *not* get home—children stuck at Ellis Island—the Y.W.C.A. gave "candy, trinkets, and small American flags," said the *Times*.

And before *that*, what was the old New York Christmas like? In 1897 Jacob Riis described "Merry Christmas in the tenements," telling of the scant greens decorating the walls where the rats scampered and the wind tore through the coverings over holes, of the poor Italian tenements where people from the same town gathered to celebrate Christmas together in dingy flats. Riis told of a creche made from a soapbox, hemlock branches and a doll, with a cardboard monkey, a Tammany tiger left over from a recent political campaign, and other makeshift creatures sitting in for the usual nativity scene animals. In the poor Syrian community close to where Battery Park City is now, the journalist found, the men visited one another with two formal kisses and the salutation "Every year and you are safe."

Thousands of single Italian, Irish, and German men took the big ocean liners docked along the wharves on the Hudson back to their native lands at the beginning of December for the holidays, carrying their bundles and the money they had saved (usually a few hundred dollars) back to their families. Then there was the scrubwomen's festival of the Tenth Ward Social Reform Club, whose president was a tenement janitress, and there was also the annual dinner for the impoverished down at the rooms of the Timothy D. ("Big Tim") Sullivan Association at 207 Bowery of turkey, beer, and the rest. A band blared Broadway tunes and there was a ritual speech by a Sullivan subordinate ("Boys"—the speaker one year was Assistant City Court Clerk—"we're all here to partake of the hospitality of Senator Timothy D. Sullivan," to which there were cries of "Hurrah, hurrah for Big Tim!"). At the dinner's conclusion, everyone got a pipe and tobacco plus a ticket to pick up waterproof shoes and wool socks at a later date. After which the next "standing" (there were no chairs) of 200 men filed in for *their* fifteen-minute repast. There was also the newsboys' dinner for the often orphaned little urchins who hawked papers in the days before newsstands and slept over gratings to keep warm. By the end of the century, the affluent came out in force to affairs where they could view the children gratefully eating the Christmas dinners provided them by various charities.

Christmas celebrations on Wall Street were cheerful in that era. The Consolidated Exchange (now defunct, then a rival to the New York Stock Exchange) took delivery of a 600-pound plum pudding the Friday before Christmas in 1909, whereupon its members dropped work to play football before polishing off the giant dessert. Observing

**ℬROKERS CAVORT ON THE FLOOR OF THE EXCHANGE
IN 1885 CHRISTMAS CELEBRATION.**

the holiday shenanigans on the Stock Exchange some years before, *Harper's Magazine* noted in 1885 that at Christmas the brokers indulged "in the blowing of tin horns and bugles, smashing of broker hats, pelting with blown bladders, wet towels and surreptitious snowballs." Holiday fun also included dropping snow or hot pennies down someone's back. Over at the Produce Exchange a few blocks away there were comic songs, followed by the giving out of "presents," e.g., "to Billy Herbert—A job to take the fat off him, Thomas Young—a position in a harem, Frank Maguire—A muzzle for Rob Marston, E.H. Moore—A book of his ancestry by Darwin," and so on.

In 1889 affluent Christmas diners at the Fifth Avenue Hotel opposite the site of what would soon be the Flatiron Building could nibble terrapin au champagne, canvasback duck, "mongrel goose," saddle of mutton, quail braisé with peas, in addition to a variety of other edibles. The Hotel Marlborough offered a menu of Massachusetts Bay oysters, followed by turtle soup, boiled chicken, beef bearnaise, lamb, diamondback terrapin, ribs, redhead duck with fried hominy and currant jelly, and so on. (The

CHRISTMAS WINDOW SHOPPING
AT THE TURN OF THE CENTURY.

following year the Murray Hill Hotel offered fillet of young bear and the Park Avenue Hotel, antelope steak.) And, oh, yes, in 1907 millionaire Harry Thaw, accused of shooting Stanford White to death on the roof of the old Madison Square Garden at 26th Street and Madison Avenue, had his second Christmas in the Tombs while awaiting trial—with a dinner of soup, blue point oysters, turkey, plum pudding, and mince pie chosen for him from Delmonico's by his wife Evelyn, née Nesbit, White's underage paramour.

So Christmas was a big deal by the early 1900s. Indeed, come Christmas in the year 1905, the editors of Mr. Pulitzer's *New York World* down on Park Row opposite City Hall requested a special Christmas story from O. Henry (or, to give him his real name, William Sydney Porter) who was then writing a short story a week for the *World*.

But the deadline for the Christmas story passed and still there was no O. Henry short story.

The illustrator went over to see O. Henry in the writer's digs at a brownstone at 55 Irving Place near Union Square—give me a story! O. Henry then gazed out the window. Go ahead with the art work, he is supposed to have said. Give me a barely furnished room with a girl with beautiful hair and a guy with a watch fob.

Days passed and there was still no story.

At the eleventh hour a reporter was sent over to lean on the writer until the story appeared. Sit on the sofa, O.Henry said, and then, supposedly modeling the hero of his story after his reluctant guest, for the next three hours wrote the story—with the aid of a large bottle of whiskey. (Perhaps for that reason, a booth at Pete's Tavern on 129 East 18th Street—in O. Henry's day, Healy's Tavern—bears an inscription saying "The Gift of the Magi" was written *there*.)

So came into being the memorable story of a young husband and wife who seemingly ruin their Christmas by each giving up what he or she loves best, he his watch fob, she her beautiful long hair, to purchase what the other most wants. The story may seem vague as to setting, but has explicit elements of New York in it—the comb that the young wife "had worshipped for long in a Broadway window" and her fear that by cutting her hair she would "look like a Coney Island chorus girl."

Yet all this Christmas hullabaloo was rather recent. Former Mayor and Congressman Smith Ely remembered around the turn of the century how "New York's celebration of Christmas is after all only a development of the past twenty years…The New York City of my early youth was distinctly a Dutch city. We had our Santa Claus to be sure and our lighted tree, but Santa Claus came on New Year's Day, and the tree was lighted a week later than it is now.

We thought little of Christmas in those days...The Puritan influence again was strong in the city, and altogether there was little popular approval of Christmas."

Indeed, sixty years or so earlier, as Mayor Ely's comments suggest, there *was* no Christmas in the sense of a national celebration with gift-giving, family reunions, Santa Claus, and all the rest. Not just New York but America, founded as it was in substantial measure by Puritans, regarded celebrations of Christmas with feasts, presents and decorations as Popish and frivolous. The well-to-do in New York and Albany gave gifts on Christmas—but only to *their servants*. Indeed, it was the existence of just such a practice of bestowing presents on the lower orders, said the *New York Herald* in 1856, which "led genteel families not to give or receive presents themselves on that day." Ahem. It was instead New Year's that was, by long European tradition, the occasion for gift-giving in New York, when friends gave gifts and merchants gave the "baker's dozen" of thirteen items to customers who had only paid for twelve.

Clement Moore had explicitly set St. Nick's gift-giving travels on Christmas Eve, of course, and this helped Christmas to slowly make headway in the New World. Still, the New Year's tradition of gift-giving died hard. For religious reasons, some strictly observant families observed Santa Claus' visit on New Year's for several more decades after Moore wrote his poem in 1822. Indeed, a mid-nineteenth century version of the famous poem was entitled, "'Twas the night before New Year's." As late as 1847, a New York City diarist noted how "New Year's presents have abounded this year." Visiting various well-endowed homes, he observed that "rich presents were displayed, from the costly cashmere shawls and silver tankard to the toy watch and child's rattle."

"NEW YEAR'S EVE" AT CANAL STREET AND BROADWAY—
IN OLD NEW YORK, THIS, RATHER THAN CHRISTMAS,
WAS THE DAY FOR PRESENTS.

New Year's

In fact, although today we think of New Year's *Eve* as the big celebratory event—in old New York it was New Year's *Day* that was the big deal. And if Christmas displaced the old New Year's Day as a time for gift-giving, New Year's Day nonetheless remained a time for young men to pay calls on all the women they knew throughout the city, a custom that by the mid 1800s had become largely identified with New York City.

"I have seen the streets of New York so packed with vehicles during the calling hours that they were blocked to all other traffic," recalled former mayor Smith Ely

147

GUY LOMBARDO, FOR DECADES MR. NEW YEAR'S EVE.

around 1900. In Edith Wharton's late novella, *New Year's Day*, the narrator recalls his boyhood in the New York City of the 1870s, when he watched from his window "the funny gentlemen who trotted about, their evening ties hardly concealed behind their overcoat collars, darting in and out of chocolate-coloured house-fronts on their sacramental round of calls." "The men boasted of the numbers of calls they made and the ladies counted up the total of their cards," recalled one real-life participant in this ritual. For a stolid party like New York diarist George Templeton Strong, thirty-some calls between 29th Street and Hudson Square between 10:45 and 5:45 on New Year's Day, 1855, "counting," he said, "cards as visits," seems to have been satisfactory.

Calling cards "bore charming winter scenes with real snow produced by ground glass," remembered a card-leaver. Some cards sprang open like accordions, others bore red lettering with gold filigree, and one apiece was to go to each young lady called upon. "As a rule the ladies received in groups, and as long as you knew one of the group, that was sufficient to justify a call." You deposited your card in the cutglass bowl provided for the purpose in the hallway, and "custom decreed that you must break bread with your hostess and partake of some liquid refreshment," a spread of punch, cookies, cakes, Madeira, and maybe more having been laid out for the anticipated guests.

THE NEW-YORK MIRROR.

SATURDAY, DECEMBER 28, 1839.

Congratulatory.—Before the next impression reaches our readers, another year will have dawned upon us, and we therefore embrace the present as the most fitting occasion we shall have of tendering our holiday congratulations both to old friends and new; and among the former there are many thousands who have been constant readers of the Mirror from its commencement, now nearly a score of years since. Among these are many whose smiles have rewarded our labours through all the vicissitudes of our editorial lifetime—we mean the ladies—God bless them!—whose bright eyes have sparkled as they looked approvingly into their Mirror. For their unchanging confidence and countenance we could say much by way of expressing our sense of gratitude, but for the present will content ourselves by wishing to one and all a cheerful, a merry, and a happy new year.

Visits on new-year's day.—We are gratified to learn that preparations are making to celebrate this good old Knickerbocker custom with greater spirit than ever on the approaching anniversary. The ladies will put on their best smiles to receive their visiters, which, with the usual adjuncts of mulled wine, coffee, and ginger-nuts, cannot fail to have an exhilarating influence upon them. We hope that this custom, which tends to strengthen friendships and keep alive the kindly feelings of the heart, may never fall into disrepute—and to the ladies we must look for its perpetuation.

Holiday presents.—The shops have put on their holiday attire. In Broadway and Chatham-street, and other parts of the town, there are splendid arrays of all descriptions of wares intended for presents. We stop to look in at the window of one of these fancy establishments—Werckmeister's. Here the lover of "little juveniles" may supply himself with hobbyhorses, regiments of infantry, squadrons of cavalry, drums, swords, trumpets, and all the accoutrements of "glorious war;" with boats, barges, steam-packets, and other nautical inventions—with tops, bats, balls, marbles, kites, sleds, and similar important trifles, or with dolls, cradles, bedsteads, and other furniture of "the baby-house," or with chairs, tables,

AN 1839 COLUMN IN THE *NEW YORK MIRROR* ENDORSES NEW YEAR'S CALLING.

ONE OF NEW YEAR'S DAY'S GENTLEMAN CALLERS—
TAKING ADVANTAGE OF THE TRADITIONAL COLLATION.

For the young men, it got to be quite a contest to see
how many calls you could make in one day, perhaps a
record being set by one John Ward and a friend on New
Year's in 1866, when they hit 107 houses, visiting seventy-
one and leaving cards at another thirty-six. They went from
Washington Square to Bond Street, then up Second Avenue
to 17th Street, over to Union Square, and then down the
East Side to 10th Street, then over to the West Side and
up to 21st Street, whence they crisscrossed Fifth Avenue
all the way up to 47th Street. Your horse could get quite
tired in the course of these lengthy rounds, so many gentlemen rented horses from a local livery stable for the day

rather than risk tuckering out their own steeds. Some hired a fancy carriage that was normally used for funerals. "Its cost was $5.00, except on New Year's when it was advanced to $6.00. This was divided pro rata among the occupants."

But the custom of New Year's Day visiting declined as the 1800s wore on. Significantly, many dutiful New Year's Day callers observed as the years passed that the city had simply grown too large for New Year's Day calling to be geographically practicable anymore. Simultaneously, the importance of New Year's *Eve* as a time of community festivity increased. By the end of the 1800s, celebrations of New Year's Eve were being held at Trinity Church at the west end of Wall Street. Here on New Year's in the early years of the twentieth century the bells were rung loudly when midnight approached as crowds gathered and a genial pandemonium broke out.

Then, in 1896, Adolph Ochs arrived in New York looking for a newspaper to buy and, finding that the one he sought was unavailable, purchased the almost moribund *New York Times* instead. At length he decided to build a new building for the *Times*, on 42nd Street. He loved putting up buildings and he wanted to showcase the *Times* so he made his new structure, at eighteen stories, one of the tallest buildings in midtown

Manhattan, at a time when most midtown structures were no more than five stories tall.

In the days before TV, video, and movies, newspapers were powerful and influential local institutions. When Joseph Pulitzer completed his new thirty-story *World* building downtown on Park Row in 1890, it was the highest building in the world, and to celebrate he hired bands, released pigeons, and rented special trains to bring in politicians from Washington. He also set off elaborate fireworks. So Ochs had a huge fireworks display when *his* building opened, too, an opening he timed to coincide with New Year's Eve. He thus in effect co-opted—or rather rerouted—the celebration that traditionally attended the coming of the New Year at Trinity Church downtown.

The next New Year's Eve he set off fireworks again. In 1907, the city forbade New Year's fireworks displays as too dangerous. So instead Ochs wowed the crowds gathered under his building with something else. He dropped a wrought iron "time" ball weighing 600 pounds from a pole atop the *Times* building to mark the exact moment when the new year began. (The idea seems to have come from the old Western Union building that stood near where the World Trade Center now is. At *exactly* noon each day, on receipt of a telegraphed signal from the Naval Observatory in Washington, a flanged-copper ball was lowered from the top of a tall pole on the building's roof. Besides advertising the telegraphic efficiency of Western Union, the precisely timed ceremony helped people check the accuracy of their pocket watches in an era before radio programs and telephone services gave the time.)

No New Year's ball was dropped in 1943 and 1944 for fear the accompanying lights would create a target for enemy pilots. Instead, prerecorded chimes were sounded at the stroke of midnight. For many years, starting with a radio broadcast in 1929, which switched over to television in 1943, the prelude to the ball's descent was the dissemination over the national airwaves of the dance tunes of Guy

New YEAR'S EVE AT TIMES SQUARE, 1953.

Lombardo and his orchestra from the Roosevelt Hotel's
Grill Room on 43rd Street and Madison Avenue and later
from the Waldorf-Astoria Hotel. Growing up in a largely
Scottish section of western Ontario, Lombardo and his
family band ended every dance, as was customary for local
bands, with the traditional favorite, "Auld Lang Syne." "We
didn't think it was known here," he later recalled. "When
we left Canada we had no idea we'd ever play it again." But
Lombardo's first radio sponsor in New York City was
Robert Burns' Panatella cigars. Since Burns had once written lyrics to "Auld Lang Syne," the band figured it would
be appropriate to close their Panatella-sponsored show
with the melody. Except among Scots, it is not clear that
"Auld Lang Syne" in this country was a New Year's Eve tradition in the first part of the century. However, when both
NBC and CBS then insisted on broadcasting Lombardo's
New Year's Eve show across the country and he played his
customary concluding tune, the nation took the Scot's song
of parting to its heart as its New Year's signature song.

Lombardo until his death in 1977 and his successor,
rock 'n' roll TV host Dick Clark (beginning in 1972 with
his "New Year's Rockin' Eve") helped transform the local
ball drop into a national and then global spectacle through
their New York City-based New Year's television specials.
Recently, Times Square has fallen under the sway of the

Times Square Business Improvement District, an organization of local businesses trying to promote the 42nd Street
area. And at the same time, the city has cracked down on
the once unruly but spontaneous gatherings that took place
in Times Square on New Year's Eve.

All of which has meant big changes for the Times
Square New Year's Eve celebration. In 1996, some 2,600
police started cordoning off the area between 57th Street
and 40th Streets on Broadway and Seventh Avenues to traffic at 7:30 p.m. and then closed the cross streets starting
at 10 p.m. The practice seems to be that the police, using
portable barriers, cordon off the crowd—about 500,000
partiers, some 85% of whom are *not* New Yorkers—with
pens and then patrol the cleared sidewalk area remaining,
confiscating any alcohol in the process.

This sets the stage for the Business Improvement District's show. As Atlanta and Miami in 1994 offered com-
peting spectacles by dropping a peach and an orange
respectively (in fairness, New York from 1981 to 1987
dropped a big apple made of red lights)—and Las Vegas
selflessly advanced the cause of American architecture in
1996 by blowing up a 900-room hotel at the stroke of
twelve—so the BID has felt obliged to tart up the New York
celebration in order to titillate the hundreds of millions of
global viewers who normally tune in the ceremony to greet

the new year. Till two years ago, for example, the ball was a modest five foot wide aluminum ball with 180 twenty-five-watt bulbs on it that was lowered on a rope by hand. Now—*now*—the ball has been souped up into a 10,000 watt xenon lamp with 12,000 rhinestones that are surrounded by 144 strobe lights and 180 halogen lights. A laser beam zaps the control system to start a computerized winch moving to lower the ball, etc., etc.

The BID also determined several years ago that the Times Square celebration was not getting *long* enough television coverage. That is, once the ball finally dropped to signal the advent of the new year, the cameras cut away. But—ah—confetti! Confetti hurled into the air takes a satisfyingly long time—several minutes, in fact—to settle. So now three thousand pounds of confetti are shot into the air at the moment the ball hits bottom to ensure that the local businesses that support the BID get the maximum TV exposure for their buck.

Which seems like a long way indeed from the celebration of the holidays in Father Knickerbocker's time. What has happened to the celebration of New Year's in New York, indeed, is perhaps emblematic of the transformation of the Christmastime holiday celebration in the city. In the 1800s Thanksgiving, Christmas, and New Year's were largely occasions for socializing among friends and family in what was then still a relatively small city. By the turn of the century, the scale of the city and also of the celebration had changed. Companies like the *New York Times*, the fashionable Fifth Avenue stores and Macy's began

TIMES SQUARE—LIGHTS, ACTION, CONFETTI!
NEW YEAR'S EVE, 1995.

to orchestrate spectacles that would appropriate the holidays for purposes of their own advertisement and glorification. Yet even the Macy's parade and the Times Square ball lowering were still predominantly New York City-oriented celebrations. Now the coming of television, global travel, and New York City's thraldom to theme enterprises like those of Disney and Warner Brothers has made these spectacles increasingly national, not to say, international foci of holiday celebration. And so they must be controlled, choreographed and, it sometimes seems, relentlessly milked for every last dollar.

And yet—"God bless us all," to coin a phrase—there remains in the midst of it a good deal of beauty, some wondrous razzle dazzle, and, sometimes all but buried underneath it all, perhaps, too, a good deal of holiday feeling.

ACKNOWLEDGMENTS: Mary A. Hernandez, Unilever United States, Inc.; Jean Hines, Cooper Hewitt Museum; The staff of the Avery and Butler Libraries at Columbia University; Jeff Campbell, Pratt Institute; The reference (and photore-production) staff of the New York Public Library, the Main and Performing Arts branches; Museum of the City of New York, Robin Feldman, Eileen Kennedy, Tony Pisani; New York Public Library Information office; Parsons School of Design Archives, Ted Barber; Macy's, Patti Schickram, Susan Hodges; Press Office, N.Y. City Ballet; Laurie Rhodes, Saks Fifth Avenue; Rockefeller Center, Sandy Manley; Keith L. Eggleston, Northeast Regional Climate Center; New York Historical Society library reference staff; Staff, Fashion Institute of Technology library; Sandra Kit, the Hayden Planetarium library; Audrey Manley, Robert Parks, The Pierpont Morgan Library; Communications Office, the American Museum of Natural History; Anne Brown, Salvation Army; Mary Barber, Debra Sanchez, Volunteers of America; Betsy Kasha, Cartier's; Christine Tripoli, Times Square Business Improvement District; Robert Norris, New York Christmas Tree Growers Association; David Spaeth, Spaeth Design; Edward Hatoff, Supervising Inspector, New York City Department of Consumer Affairs; Margaret Ternes, Park Avenue Holiday Lighting, Inc.; Sunny Lebowitz, Lord & Taylor; Craig Evans, Salvation Army; Deborah McLauchlan; Michael LeCompte; Ms. Linn Howard; Gentry Johns, New York City Visitors and Convention Bureau; Public Affairs Division, New York City Department of Transportation; Margaret Kaplan, Joan Siebert, Harry N. Abrams, Inc.; Beth Barbary, Barbara Horgan, The George Balanchine Trust; L. Johnson, Wesleyan University Cinema Archives; Sony Corporation; Michelle Kerr, Barnard College Public Relations; Barnard College Archives; Deanna Cross, Metropolitan Museum of Art; General Theological Seminary; Kathy Dawkins, Department of Sanitation; David Murbach, director of horticulture, Rockefeller Center; Stephen Fybish; Professor Jeffrey Miller; Eugene Pool, *il miglior fabbro*.

Group, Inc. **PAGE 42:** The City's Christmas Tree, 1913. Madison Square Park. Drawn by Carlton Moorepark. Museum of the City of New York. Gift of Mrs. William B. Isham. **PAGE 45:** William Rivelli. **PAGE 49:** William Rivelli. **PAGE 50:** Helayne Seidman. **PAGE 52:** John Sotomayor/NYT Pictures. **PAGE 53:** William Rivelli. **PAGE 56:** William Rivelli. **PAGE 58:** Courtesy of Douglas Leigh. **PAGE 59:** William Rivelli. **PAGE 61:** William Rivelli. **PAGE 62:** Photographer unkown. **PAGE 63:** 1996 holiday windows at the Sony Style Store in New York created by Maurice Sendak. **PAGE 68:** Salvation Army Christmas Dinner Kettle, 1906. Museum of the City of New York. The Byron Collection. 93.1.1.17268. **PAGE 73:** Jennifer Weisbord. **PAGE 76:** The New York Times/NYT Pictures. **PAGE 78:** Portrait painted late in life for the General Theological Seminary. **PAGE 79:** © Collection of the New York Historical Society. **PAGE 86:** By Paul Kolnik. THE NUTCRACKER choreography by George Balanchine © The BALANCHINE Trust. THE NUTCRACKER℠ The George Balanchine Trust. Balanchine® is a Registered Trade Mark of the George Balanchine Trust. **PAGE 88:** Andrea Mohin/NYT Pictures. **PAGE 92:** Photo by George Kalinsky. Madison Square Garden Productions. **PAGE 95:** The New York Times/NYT Pictures. **PAGE 99:** Courtesy National Choral Council. **PAGE 102:** William Rivelli. **PAGE 105:** William Rivelli. **PAGE 108:** Courtesy Unilever United States, Inc. **PAGE 109:** Billy Rose Theatre Collection, Vandam Collection. The New York Public Library for the Performing Arts. Astor, Lenox, and Tilden Foundations. **PAGE 112:** Ernst Beadle. **PAGE 115:** Metropolitan Museum of Art, Gift of Loretta Hines Howard, 1964. (64.164.167). Detail. **PAGE 118:** Neg. No. 65980 (fr. 36). Photo by Jim Coxe. Courtesy Dept. of Library Services, American Museum of Natural History. **PAGE 119:** Neg. No. 2A 18885. Photo by D. Finnin. Courtesy Dept. of Library Services, American Museum of Natural History. **PAGE 122:** Wesleyan University Cinema Archives. **PAGE 126:** Courtesy *Musical America*. **PAGE 130:** The Kobal Collection. Courtesy 20th Century Fox. **PAGE 134:** General Research Division. The New York Public Library. Astor-Lenox-Tilden Foundations. **PAGE 136:** Barnard College Archives. **PAGE 140:** Christmas Carnival in the New York Stock Exchange. c. 1885. Museum of the City of New York. Gift of Miss Grace M. Mayer. **PAGE 141:** General Research Division. The New York Public Library. Astor-Lenox-Tilden Foundations. **PAGE 145:** New Year's Eve c. 1865. (Scene at Broadway and Canal Street). Lithograph colored. Artist: F. Fuchs. Publishers: Kimmel & Foster. Museum of the City of New York. 29.100.2767. **PAGE 146:** Archive Photos. **PAGE 149:** Holiday Article. *The New York Mirror*. Saturday, December 28, 1838. Museum of the City of New York. **PAGE 150:** General Research Division. The New York Public Library. Astor-Lenox-Tilden Foundations. **PAGE 153:** The New York Times/NYT Pictures. **PAGE 157:** Donal Holway.

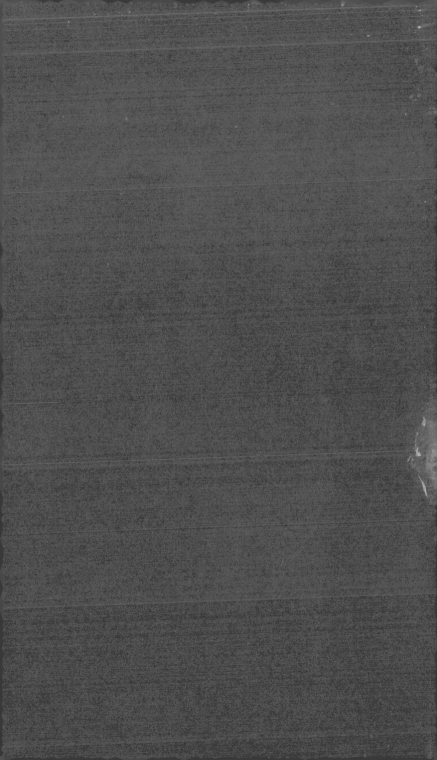